PREFACE

"The Making of the American Constitution" has been a continuous process ever since the eighteenth century, but this book is concerned solely with the orgins of the Constitution and with its writing and adoption; only incidentally is there any reference to the evolution of the Constitution since 1789. Men in eighteenth-century America looked upon society and government in a way not always relished by more romantically inclined later generations. Nevertheless, I think it is worthwhile to attempt to see eighteenth-century problems as men of that century saw them. Therefore, this book is based upon the debates in the Philadelphia Convention and the state ratifying conventions, and upon the newspapers and private letters of the period.

Naturally, much has had to be omitted. Innumerable relevant qualifications have been omitted, scores of controverted issues have received all too brief mention, and many a generalization of a sentence or two has had to stand in place of an extended discussion. However, it is my hope that the book does present the major issues (as seen at the time) involved in the most important political and constitutional decision in the history of the United States.

MERRILL JENSEN

Madison, Wisconsin

THE MAKING OF
THE AMERICAN
CONSTITUTION

MERRILL JENSEN
Professor of History
University of Wisconsin

AN ANVIL ORIGINAL
under the general editorship of
LOUIS L. SNYDER

D. VAN NOSTRAND COMPANY, INC.
PRINCETON, NEW JERSEY
TORONTO   NEW YORK   LONDON

TO

JAMES MADISON

D. VAN NOSTRAND COMPANY, INC.
120 Alexander St., Princeton, New Jersey (*Principal office*); 24 West 40 St., New York, N.Y.
D. VAN NOSTRAND COMPANY (Canada), LTD.
25 Hollinger Rd., Toronto 16, Canada
D. VAN NOSTRAND COMPANY, LTD.
358, Kensington High Street, London, W.14, England

PRINTED IN THE UNITED STATES OF AMERICA

TABLE OF CONTENTS

Part I

THE MAKING OF
THE CONSTITUTION

— 1 —

INTRODUCTION

Few statesmen in American history have had such an extraordinary combination of experience, education, and talent as the group of men who wrote the Constitution of the United States in Philadelphia during the long, hot summer of 1787. The delegates were men of great political skill, trained in the rough but effective school provided by the age of the American Revolution. A few began political careers before the onset of the revolutionary crisis in 1763, more rose to eminence between 1763 and 1774, and a remarkable group of younger men got started during the war itself. Some of the delegates had helped write the first state constitutions and the first constitution of the United States, the Articles of Confederation. Most of them had taken part in political battles in Congress and in the states as governors, judges, and legislators. By 1787, virtually all of them were convinced that alterations must be made in the constitutions of the states and of the United States.

Yet most of the members of the Convention, before 1787 at least, were not professional politicians in any latter-day sense. They had been and continued to be, first of all, planters, merchants, and professional men for whom political activity was a responsibility (and sometimes an opportunity) added to their major concerns. As a group they were, in fact or by inclination, members of the economic, social, and intellectual aristocracies of their respective states, not of the small farmer and artisan classes which made up the great bulk of the American population. Furthermore, they took it for granted that society was divided into classes—that it always had been and always would be—and that the principal object of government was the adjustment of the conflicting interests of classes in any political society.

The members of the Convention shared a common education that was centered around the history and political philosophy of the ancient world and of England. As a result, some of them believed that they could draw upon the history of the past, in fact must draw upon it, if they were to achieve a workable constitution. Thus James Madison spent a part of the winter before the Convention studying the constitutions of ancient and modern confederacies, while in Europe John Adams outlined the history of a host of past states to set forth their defects and the causes of their fall.

The lesson of history was clear and the outcome inevitable. History taught, such men believed, that there were only three kinds of government—monarchy, aristocracy, and democracy—and that each had fatal defects. They believed too that if any one class in society got control of government, it would exploit all the others. The solution, so political theorists ever since Aristotle had taught, was a "balanced government" in which each class in society was represented and given a check upon the others to protect its interests. The history they read and believed showed that every democracy in the past had ended in class warfare between the poor and the rich. As John Adams put it: "There never was a democracy that did not commit suicide."

The delegates recognized that the United States in 1787 did not suffer from the maldistribution of property which had characterized ancient states and which was true of contemporary Europe. But they believed it inevitable that in the future the United States would become like every other state in history, and that the majority of the American people would, in time, be without property. Experience since 1776 demonstrated, so more than one delegate said, that the American state governments were too democratic. The task before the delegates was, therefore, a double one: to check the "levelling spirit" which, they believed, had arisen since 1776, and to provide protection for property in that future time when property owners would be a minority in the United States. It was in such specific terms that James Madison explained what the Convention should do, and no delegate disagreed with him.

There were men in the Convention, and Madison was one, who also thought in terms of "national character," but they were not the majority. When the Convention was over, Madison himself declared that "the mutability of the laws of the states" and the evils arising from them had "contributed more to that uneasiness which produced the Convention, and prepared the public mind for a general reform, than those which accrued to our national character and interest from the inadequacy of the Confederation to its immediate objects." The relevance of this judgment was illustrated by James Wilson's comment concerning the restraints placed upon the state governments by the Constitution. "If only the following lines were inserted in this Constitution," he said, "I think it would be worth our adoption." He cited the provisions forbidding the states to issue paper money, to make anything but gold and silver coin legal tender in payment of debts, or to pass bills of attainder, ex post facto laws, and laws impairing the obligation of contracts. "How insecure is property!" he concluded. And once ratification had been achieved, Madison, in effect, agreed with Wilson. He sent Jefferson a pamphlet containing the amendments proposed by the state ratifying conventions. They omitted, he declared, "many of the true grounds of opposition. The articles relating to treaties, to paper money, and to contracts created more enemies than all the errors in the system, positive and negative, put together."

The interpretation of history accepted by Madison and other members of the Convention, their analysis of and their proposed solution for the problem as they saw it, and their predictions about the future history of the United States may all have been mistaken. But right or wrong, it was within the framework of such ideas that they operated. Only if we understand their assumptions can we understand much of what they tried to do. Their common heritage of education, political experience, and constitutional and political ideas was so taken for granted that they found little need to discuss it. Hence they spent most of their time debating details, many of which they disagreed about bitterly. But the great majority of the Convention did not disagree about ultimate goals. It was because they agreed about ends that they adopted one compromise and political bargain after another whenever it seemed that the Convention might break up in bitter disputes over means.

One must, therefore, begin with the heritage of political experience and ideas which did so much to shape the final outcome. It is only within this context that we can understand the debates in the Convention which wrote, and the state conventions which adopted, the Constitution of the United States.

— 2 —

THE COLONIAL BACKGROUND

The Heritage of Ideas.   The Americans of the revolutionary generation were the heirs of the political and constitutional ideas of the mother country and the products of a century and a half of experience as members of the British Empire. They were fully aware of the "rights of Englishmen," with which no government should be allowed to interfere, and of the "rights of Englishmen" when sitting as members of a legislature. The ideas that each Englishman should be free from arrest and imprisonment except upon a definite charge and by due process of law, have the right to a trial by jury of his equals from the vicinity in which he lived, be exempt from taxation except by the vote of elected representatives, and have the right to petition for a redress of grievances—all were brought to America by the English colonists and were guaranteed to them in every colonial charter.

The ideas that members of a legislature should be free from interference in elections, be free from arrest and have freedom of speech during sessions of the legislature, and have the sole right to levy taxes were likewise brought to America. The colonists sympathized with the Parliament in England that fought for the rights of Englishmen as men and as legislators during the seventeenth century and achieved a final triumph over the Crown in the Glorious Revolution of 1688-1689. These ideas, embodied in such documents as the Petition of Right in 1628 and the Bill of Rights in 1689, were as close to the hearts of Americans as of Englishmen and found expression in the constitutions that Americans wrote during the age of the American Revolution.

Americans were the heirs, too, of a body of ideas stemming from the Protestant Reformation in England. A left wing of the Puritan movement held that the only true church was a voluntary association of like-minded believers. In time such people came to the conclusion that the only true state was a similar thing, and some of them made their way to the English colonies and established governments for themselves. Contrary to the assumption of English authorities who held that no colonial government had any legal validity unless based upon a royal charter, such religious groups believed that a people, by a voluntary association, could create a valid government, as did those in Plymouth, Connecticut, and Rhode Island. It was but one step from the idea of voluntary association as the basis of government to the doctrine of the sovereignty of the people—of democracy— a step taken explicitly by the people of Rhode Island. These ideas of the right of voluntary association and of democracy were to be the theoretical foundation of the war for American independence and were expressed in enduring form in the Declaration of Independence.

The Heritage of Political Institutions. The heritage of political and constitutional ideas from England might have meant little if the colonists had not possessed a political institution through which such ideas could be asserted and maintained. But the English colonists did acquire such an institution, the elective legislature. Its establishment was an accident of history, not the result of any plan on the part of the English government. The Virginia Company looked upon its colonists in Virginia as members of the company, and in 1619 it authorized the governor to call together representatives of the plantations to make laws for their own government. When the House of Burgesses met, it at once began acting like a legislature, for it was aware of parliamentary traditions, and within a short time it was claiming the sole right to levy taxes in the colony. The company's charter was revoked in 1624, and the government of the colony was taken over by the king. Fifteen years later Charles I recognized the institution established by the Virginia Company, and thereafter a representative legislature was an integral part of the government of Virginia. The precedent, once established, was applied to colonies founded thereafter. Meanwhile, the New England colonies, founded by religious groups, had established elected legislatures as a matter of course.

Once established, the existence of colonial legislatures was never challenged successfully. James II did eliminate the New England legislatures after he became king in 1685, but he was driven from his throne in the Glorious Revolution of 1688-1689, and the legislatures were reestablished at once. Thereafter, England tried to bring the colonies under closer control by converting them into royal colonies administered directly by the Crown. The result of this policy was that by 1775 only Connecticut and Rhode Island remained as self-governing corporations, and only Pennsylvania, Delaware, and Maryland as proprietary colonies. But however much English officials might quarrel with the legislatures and deplore their growing power, they never sought to abolish them.

The legislatures were only a part of the structure of colonial governments. The colonies had been founded by private groups and individuals with aims ranging all the way from the creation of authoritarian religious commonwealths through self-governing democracies to feudal societies in the wilderness. The early forms of government were consequently quite different. Yet by the end of the seventeenth century, partly as a result of English policy and partly as a result of the determination of the colonists, the structure of government in each colony was much like that of the others. That structure remained unchanged during the eighteenth century and was taken over intact by the Americans when they wrote their first state constitutions after 1775.

At the head of each government was a governor, appointed by the Crown in the royal colonies, by the proprietors in the proprietary colonies, and elected in Connecticut and Rhode Island. In all but the last two colonies, the governors had great legal powers derived from the commissions given them by the Crown and the proprietors.

The governors appointed most of the officials in each colony: judges, militia officers, sheriffs, and the like. They could call, dissolve, and delay or suspend sessions of the legislatures at will, and they had an absolute veto over legislation. In the royal colonies the governors enjoyed vast social prestige as direct representatives of the Crown. But a governor's power was limited by the facts of politics. Each had a council whose advice and consent was necessary for political appointments and for vetoes of legislation. The councilors in the royal colonies were appointed by the Crown and invariably were chosen from among the wealthy and politically prominent men. Most councilors were, therefore, what amounted to political "bosses," and a governor was forced to work with them if he was to succeed at all. But above all, a governor's success was dependent upon his ability to persuade the elected branch of the legislature to provide money for the operations of government, and usually for his own salary as well. His theoretically great power was therefore sharply limited in practice. It was an awareness of both the theory and the reality that did much to shape American thinking about the role of the executive when they wrote their state and federal constitutions after 1775.

The second part of the structure with which Americans were familiar as they wrote their constitutions was the council. In every colony except Pennsylvania, the council had served as the upper house of the legislature as well as an advisory body to the governor. In Virginia, the governor and council were, in addition, the supreme court of the colony. The councilors were elected only in

Massachusetts, Connecticut, and Rhode Island, but even in those colonies councilors usually held office for life. The councils were in fact if not in name the equivalent of the House of Lords in England; they were expected to serve as a check on the supposedly less stable elected branches of the legislatures. It was this function that was in the mind of many Americans as they drafted their state constitutions, and it was discussed at length in the creation of the senate during the Convention of 1787.

Despite the power of the governor and the fact that the councils, on the whole, represented the wealthier and more conservative classes of colonial society, the weight of power lay with the elected branches—the colonial assemblies. They self-consciously modeled their procedure on that of the House of Commons in England, used the precedents it had established, and made the same claims to power. Their major weapon was the same: the "power of the purse." The operations of the colonial governments depended upon the taxes raised, and those taxes were voted by the legislatures. The elected branches insisted that they alone had the right to initiate tax legislation and to control the spending of the money raised, whatever the legal power of the governor or the legislative rights of the councils. The assemblies used this power to check governors, to direct their appointments to office, and even to deprive them of their authority as commanders of military forces. Bit by bit the elected assemblies acquired more power until by mid-eighteenth century most of them had gained almost complete control over the internal affairs of the colonies. This was a fact recognized by the assemblies, by despairing colonial governors, and by officials in England. The legislative supremacy thus achieved was formalized in the first constitutions of the American states.

Despite the achievement of self-government internally, the colonies were still a part of the British Empire. The government of the colonies was not two systems—colonial and British—but one interlocking system with final legal authority located in London. The Americans, therefore, had experience with a central government long before they wrote the constitution of a central government for themselves. The government of the empire was in fact a vast "federal" structure. It was awkward, un-

wieldy, and often unworkable, but many of its devices
for achieving centralized control were to be written into
the Constitution of 1787.

The first colonies were founded before England had
a colonial policy, and when she began to develop one
after 1660, she was faced with the fact that many of
the basic patterns of colonial political and economic life
were already established. The development of a colonial
policy followed upon the realization that colonies were
becoming economically important. By 1660 the growing
production of Virginia and Maryland tobacco and West
Indian sugar gave rise to demands that colonial trade
be confined to England. The resulting Acts of Trade and
Navigation, passed between 1660 and 1696, required that
all goods shipped to and from the colonies must be carried in English or colonial ships; that certain colonial
products such as sugar and tobacco could be shipped
only to England or to another English colony; and that
the colonies must buy manufactured goods from England,
or if foreign, such goods must be shipped through England. A corollary, spelled out by later legislation, was
that the colonies must not manufacture anything that
would compete with English industry.

Policy was established by Parliament, but administration of policy was in the hands of the Crown, for
the colonies, legally, were the domain of the monarch.
The king, meeting with his Privy Council, was the administrative head of the empire, and in the course of
time a host of administrative boards and officials in England and in America were established to carry out the
policies established by Parliament. The evolution of a
great and overlapping bureaucracy led to confusion, in-
action, and uncertainty as to what policy really was, for
often the laws themselves were subject to many interpretations. Furthermore, America was a long way from
the center of the empire, and the colonists often found
it easy to evade policies they did not like.

The development of an economic policy was accompanied by the growth of political devices to bring the
colonies under closer administrative control. One such
device was the conversion of semi-independent corpora-
tion and proprietary colonies into royal colonies, thus
giving the Crown and its agents the power to appoint

governors, judiciaries, and upper houses of legislatures. A second device was the appeal of cases from colonial supreme courts to the monarch's Privy Council in England, which thus functioned as the supreme court of the empire. More and more cases were appealed during the eighteenth century despite the protests of the colonial supreme courts. A third device to achieve closer control was the royal disallowance of colonial legislation—a veto by the Privy Council in the name of the king—which was often used, particularly in the attempt to limit or block colonial legislation issuing paper money. When this failed, as it did in the case of paper money, Parliament was called in to forbid the issue of legal tender paper, as it did for New England in 1751 and for the rest of the colonies in 1764.

Each of these devices used by the British government to achieve closer control over the colonies—appointment of local officials, review of cases by a supreme court, veto of the acts of local legislatures, and restraints upon their economic activities—were suggested by the writers of the Constitution of 1787, and a number of them found their way into the final draft of that document. From a strictly constitutional view, therefore, the war for independence was merely an interlude. Great Britain tried to achieve a truly centralized empire in fact as well as in theory after 1763, and she lost the thirteen colonies as a result. The writers of the Constitution succeeded where Britain had failed, and they went farther than she had tried to go before 1775, although not as far as many of them wanted to in 1787.

THE CONSTITUTIONAL DEBATE AND REVOLUTIONARY CONSTITUTION MAKING, 1763-1783

The Debate with Britain. The constitutional debate was carried on at two levels: between Britain and the colonies concerning the nature of the constitution of the empire, and among Americans themselves concerning the basis and purpose of government. The debate with Britain was in a real sense the same argument that had been going on ever since the beginnings of English colonial policy in the seventeenth century. After 1763, however, it was carried on with an intensity never before equalled. The reasons for British policies after 1763 and for American reactions to them were many and complex—economic, social, political, and personal—but the constitutional issue was simple. Parliament had been passing laws affecting the colonies for more than a century, but after 1763 it tried for the first time to raise money in the colonies by direct taxation.

The attempt was a denial of the most cherished claim of every colonial legislature, for Americans insisted that they could not be taxed except by representatives of their own choosing. They effectively nullified the Stamp Act in 1765, but when Parliament repealed the act in 1766 it stated its position in the Declaratory Act and did not retreat from it until after the war for American independence began. Parliament asserted that it had the right to legislate for the colonies "in all cases whatsoever" and thus proclaimed itself an absolute central government. In theory the Declaratory Act wiped out the federal structure which had long existed in practice and asserted that the empire was a unitary state.

The Americans' answer was equally simple. Within a short time they worked out what has been called the "commonwealth" theory of the empire, which was essentially a rationalization or formulation of the practice of the past. This theory held that the empire was made up of separate segments, each with an independent and equal legislature. Parliament was the legislature of Great Britain, the House of Burgesses the legislature of Virginia, and neither had any authority over the other. The common bond of the empire was the monarch, who should act as an umpire when interests clashed.

The insistence on the independence and equality of each of the legislatures within the empire was heartily supported by leaders of the American revolutionary movement and by their followers. And this conviction, carried over into the new nation after 1776, had a profound impact on the writing of the first state constitutions. The conviction was likewise a major obstacle to the creation of a central government in the United States with any power at all over the separate and independent states and their citizens.

The Debate Among Americans.   The second phase of the revolutionary debate was among Americans over the origin, nature, and ultimate purpose of government. While colonial legislatures and many American leaders were arguing with Great Britain about taxation and charter rights, others were appealing to "natural rights," "natural law," and the "law of nature." They elaborated on the idea of the compact theory of government and proclaimed the idea that all government is based upon the consent of the people governed. Legislators in conspicuous positions did not often appeal to such ideas, but anonymous newspaper writers did, and their ideas were taken up by local political bodies. Thus in 1765 in New London, Connecticut, a mass meeting proclaimed that every form of government, rightly founded, originates in the consent of the people, and concluded that if relief from the Stamp Act could be obtained in no other way, the people should "resume their natural rights and the authority the laws of nature and of God had vested them with."

Americans also agreed that there should be single written constitutions because they had always been familiar with them in the form of colonial charters, "frames" of government such as those of Pennsylvania, and the commissions of royal governors which were, in effect, the constitutions of the royal colonies. Americans were agreed, too, on keeping the familiar structure of the colonial governments, but they disagreed about the ends of government, and above all about the balance of power within the formal structure which they carried over intact from colonial times.

One group demanded that the new state governments be democratic and asserted that democracy was the best form of government to achieve the happiness of the people which was defined as the end of all government. The constitutions proposed called for one- or two-house legislatures elected by the people annually; the election of all public officials by the people or by the legislatures; the right to vote for every adult male, or at least for all those who bore arms; representation according to population; and religious freedom, or at least the abolition of state churches and taxes paid by all to support them.

Some of these ideas were old ones, but their reiteration in 1776 shocked many American leaders who feared revolution within America if independence were declared. Some of them, therefore, opposed independence, although most of them became patriots when forced to choose. But they did not accept the democratic ideas let loose by independence, and they opposed any fundamental change in the basic political structure of American society. Yet, separation from Great Britain made change inevitable, for some new means had to be found of naming the hierarchy of governors, upper houses, judiciaries, and local officials, most of whom had been appointed directly or indirectly by Great Britain. Even if there had been no other political changes, this alone constituted a political revolution.

The State Constitutions. While the new state constitutions retained the formal structure of the colonial governments, there was a radical shift in the balance of power within that structure. The state constitutions reduced the governor to a mere figurehead with no power over the legislature. Ten states required annual election, and in seven of them the governor could serve no more than two or three years out of any six. In addition, most constitutions created a council whose permission was necessary before the governor could take any action. The old legislative function of the colonial council was handed over to a senate which in some states was looked upon as representing wealth. But even so, the senates were now subject to the will of the voters as the councils had never been. The courts too came within the indirect control of the voters. Judges were now elected by the legislatures or appointed by governors who in turn were elected by the legislatures or by the voters.

The assemblies became the dominant branch of each state government in law as well as in fact. They retained all their old powers and added new ones, including the power, in some states, to elect governors and other officials. Their power over taxation and other economic legislation was now absolute, and in some states the senates were forbidden to amend money bills. While the assemblies had to share power with the senates in elections of governors and judges, and the senates also had to pass legislation, the members of the assemblies were more numerous and could usually subdue a recalcitrant senate. And, as never before, the assemblies were closer to the electorate because of annual elections and the ever-present possibility of a quick overturn if the representatives did not respect the voters' wishes.

In addition to providing a revolutionary change in the balance of power within government, many of the new state constitutions embodied the more striking ideals of the revolutionary age in bills of rights. Such bills restated the rights and privileges of individuals with which no government might interfere. These were a part of the English heritage, long a part of American thought and feeling. But other ideas were added. Thus, many of the bills included specific statements of the sovereignty of the people and of their right to change their governments at will. Some of them contained eloquent proclamations of the right to freedom of religion, to freedom of the press, and to freedom to think as one pleased. Some of the bills contained explicit statements of the idea of state sovereignty—that the state was to retain all power not specifically delegated to the Congress of the United States. These statements of state sovereignty reflect the distrust of centralized, uncontrolled governmental power which was so basic a part of the political thought of the times and which had been given point by Parliament's assumption of absolute power in the Declaratory Act of 1766. It reflected, too, the intensity of what should be called the "national feeling" of the people for their own states rather than for the new entity known as the United States.

— 4 —

THE FIRST CONSTITUTION OF THE UNITED STATES—THE ARTICLES OF CONFEDERATION

The Idea of Union Before 1776. The political ideas and attitudes so clearly expressed in the first state constitutions had an inescapable impact on the first constitution of the United States—the Articles of Confederation. Americans in 1776 were thoroughly familiar with the idea of a central government, for the British government had been such throughout their history. They were familiar too with the idea of a central government within America itself. During the eighteenth century both Americans and Englishmen had offered plans for a colonial union consisting of a congress elected by the legislatures and an executive appointed by the Crown. The purpose of the early plans was to provide for more effective defense against the French and Indians in Canada, but in 1754 the Albany Plan of Union proposed that the central government be given power to tax and to control western lands, as well as power over military affairs. Every colonial legislature that considered the plan rejected it flatly. They no more wanted any limitation on their power by an American legislature than they did by that of Great Britain.

After 1763, support for the idea of colonial union came from two sources. It came first of all from the popular leaders who opposed British policies, men who were convinced that effective opposition was possible only if the colonies took united action. But such leaders offered no plans for a common colonial government. Plans were offered instead by more conservative Americans who were alarmed by the growth of extra-legal action and the spread of democratic ideas. A "supreme legislature," said the supporter of one such plan, should have the power to make laws for the "internal police" of the colonies and thus would have a "tendency of checking a turbulent spirit in any one of the colonies. . . ." In the First Continental Congress, Joseph Galloway offered a plan of union to counter the "republicans" whom he was certain were bent on independence. He argued that there must be a supreme legislature in every society and that both political units and individuals must be subordinated to it. If Parliament were denied power over the colonies, then there must be an American legislature to regulate trade and prevent the colonies from going to war with one another. Galloway's proposal was rejected by the popular leaders, and all mention of it was erased from the published journals.

But by spring 1775 and early 1776 the popular leaders supported the idea of a union as a means of moving the colonies toward independence, while the men who had supported Galloway's plan now opposed union because of its purpose. But when they saw that independence could no longer be avoided, they again reversed themselves and insisted that there must be a constitutional union of the colonies before independence was declared. They argued that there would be anarchy without such a union, that there would be civil war between states over boundaries, that centralized regulation of trade was necessary, and centralized control over western lands as well.

When Richard Henry Lee moved on June 7, 1776, that Congress declare independence, he also moved that there be a committee to draft articles of confederation. The committee was appointed at once with John Dickinson, the leader of the opposition to independence and the strongest spokesman for a strong central government, as chairman. On July 12, ten days after Congress voted for Lee's motion on independence, the committee presented the draft of a federal constitution to Congress.

The Forces For and Against Union After 1776. The Americans had many things in common that aided in the formation of a central government: a common language, common political ideas and institutions, and above all, the necessity of fighting a war to make good the independence they had declared. Furthermore, each state had within it men who were convinced there must be a central government with sovereign power over the states and their citizens, a government which could regulate trade, control western lands, limit paper money issues, and interfere within states to suppress internal rebellions. This conviction was expressed before independence, during the war, and after it, until in 1787 they were able to achieve a measure of what they wanted.

There were equally strong forces working against the creation of a strong central government. While the people of the states had much in common, there was much that was different in social structure, religion, and economic interests. New Englanders believed that the southerners were too aristocratic, and the southerners thought that the New Englanders were dangerously democratic. Merchants of various states were rivals, and the southern planters disliked merchants as a class. There were conflicts between states over boundaries which had actually led to armed clashes in 1774 and 1775. Virginia's neighbors feared that she might swallow them up, while throughout America Bostonians were suspected of being hypocrites and dangerous men.

The attachment of citizens to their states was deep and was expressed in the state constitutions. The idea that each colonial government was independent of all outside control had been dinned into American ears ever since 1763, and it is little wonder that the majority of the people believed in it by 1776. By and large this was the view, too, of the popular leaders of the revolutionary movement who sprang to the fore after 1763. Such leaders agreed that there must be a central government, but they did not want a government that could interfere with either the states or their citizens. They wanted, in fact, a government subordinate to the states and controlled by them. Their view had been fortified by the struggle against Parliament, and it was bolstered too by certain political ideas which they all accepted. They agreed with eighteenth-century English writers, such as James Burgh, that political power had a dangerous impact on the minds and behavior of men in office: that the possession of power created the desire for ever more power. As Burgh put it, "the love of power is natural, it is insatiable; it is whetted, not cloyed, by possession."

It was this distrust of men in power and of power seekers that explains the emphasis on annual elections and rotation in office in the state constitutions. The idea was embodied in the Maryland bill of rights, which asserted that "a long continuance in the first executive departments of power or trust, is dangerous to liberty; a rotation, therefore in those departments, is one of the best securities of permanent freedom." It was this conviction on the part of many revolutionary leaders which led them to oppose the creation of a central government far removed from the control of the voters, and with power over them. It was this feeling that gave rise to one of the most remarkable self-denying ordinances in the history of written constitutions. The Articles of Confederation provided that no man could be a member of the Congress of the United States for more than three years out of any six.

The Major Issues.   The draft of articles of confederation presented to Congress on July 12, 1776, was largely the work of John Dickinson, one of the subtlest legal minds of the time. That draft provided the legal basis for a powerful central government. First, it offered only one guarantee of the power of the states—control of their internal police (that is, internal affairs), but the guarantee was sharply limited to only those matters which would not interfere with the powers of Congress. Second, it placed only one limitation on the power of Congress—it could not levy taxes or duties except to maintain a postoffice.

The significance of this basic fact was not realized at first because of more obvious issues. These issues were debated hotly in 1776 and 1777, and they were to be debated again in the Convention of 1787 when some of the same men were to use the same arguments they had used 11 years before. In 1776 the large and small states battled over "representation," with the large states insisting on votes in Congress according to population and the small states insisting on equal votes for each state. The small states won in 1776 simply because they outnumbered the large states. A second issue, this time between the northern and southern states, was the basis for paying common expenses. The northern states supported Dickinson's proposal that expenses be apportioned according to population. The southern states insisted that their slaves could not be counted because they were property. They proposed instead that expenses be shared according to the value of granted and improved lands within each state, and they won out over the northern states. The way in which slaves were to be counted was to be an issue 11 years later as well.

The bitterest issue in writing the Articles of Confederation was the control of western lands. Dickinson gave it to the central government. He was supported by the states with definite western boundaries—Pennsylvania, Maryland, New Jersey, Delaware, and Rhode Island—and opposed by all the others which had charter claims of some sort running to the "South Seas." Behind the attempt to give Congress control of the West was the fear of Virginia's vast claims and the power they would give her. Behind it, too, were the ambitions of land speculators from the landless states, who stood little chance of realizing their hopes if the most desirable areas west of the Appalachians remained in Virginia's hands. In fact, individual land speculators and companies produced some of the most ingenious legal and constitutional theories of the times to prove that Congress was a sovereign government and hence one with the power to deprive Virginia of her lands. Only thus could such speculators hope to share in the land beyond the mountains from which many Americans of the time hoped to make fortunes.

Virginia and other landed states were outraged by the Dickinson proposal. They removed it from the Articles and added a provision that no state could be deprived of land without its consent. It was this issue that held up ratification of the Articles of Confederation until March 1781. Virginia declared void the speculative land claims of such men as Robert Morris, James Wilson, Benjamin

Franklin, and several Maryland political leaders within her asserted boundaries. She then ceded her claims northwest of the Ohio to Congress, and Maryland, which had held out longest, was at last forced to ratify. But this bitter dispute, like many others, was to be renewed in the Convention of 1787.

The overriding issue in 1776-1777, as in 1787, was that of sovereignty: the location of ultimate constitutional power in the United States. By implication and omission, the Dickinson draft gave it to the central government, but no one realized it until the spring of 1777, when Dr. Thomas Burke of North Carolina told Congress that the draft provided the legal basis for a central government of almost unlimited power. He was opposed by James Wilson of Pennsylvania, who throughout the Revolution, in the Convention of 1787, and as an associate justice of the United States Supreme Court after 1789, was one of the most consistent supporters of a strong central government. During 1776 and 1777, Wilson tried repeatedly to establish precedents upon the basis of which Congress might acquire more power, and he now tried to obscure the issue raised by Burke. But again he failed. Burke subscribed completely to the doctrine that men in power could not be trusted. His formulation was that "power of all kinds has an irresistible propensity to increase a desire for itself." To check this appetite he proposed an amendment to the Dickinson draft which changed its fundamental character, and 11 states voted for it. As the second article of the Articles of Confederation, it reads:

Each state retains its sovereignty, freedom, and independence, and every power, jurisdiction, and right which is not by this confederation expressly delegated to the United States in Congress assembled.

This amendment (which reflected provisions in several state bills of rights) guaranteed that the central government would have only specifically delegated powers and that the states would retain all others. The concept remained a living force. In 1787-1788 there was such a widespread demand for adding the same amendment to the Constitution, that, in weakened form, it became a part of the Bill of Rights as the tenth amendment.

The Character of the Articles.   The Articles of Confederation provided for a strictly federal government representing equal states which elected the members of Congress and recalled them at will. Nevertheless, the constitution included many principles and provisions which were taken over by the constitution makers in 1787, and considering the strong opposition to centralization, it contains a remarkable list of restraints upon the states and assigns a remarkable number of duties and powers to Congress.

The citizens of a state were guaranteed the privileges of the citizen of any state to which they might go. The extradition of criminals was provided for. Each state was required to give "full faith and credit" to the judicial proceedings of every other state. No state could make foreign alliances without the consent of Congress. No persons holding offices of trust in the states or in Congress could receive gifts or titles from foreign states, and Congress and the states were forbidden to grant titles of nobility. The states could not levy tariffs interfering with the treaties of the United States, nor maintain military and naval forces in peacetime except those judged necessary by Congress. Nor could the states engage in war without the consent of Congress, except in the case of sudden invasion.

Congress was given a long list of powers and duties in foreign, domestic, and military affairs. It had the power to make peace and war, send and receive ambassadors, make treaties, and appoint courts to try cases of disputes over captures at sea.

In military affairs, Congress had the power to appoint all officers of land and sea forces (except regimental officers), to direct the operations of both land and naval forces, and to build and equip a navy.

In domestic affairs, Congress had the power to regulate the value of coins minted by it and the states, to issue paper money, to borrow money, to establish weights and measures, to establish and regulate postoffices throughout the United States, to regulate trade with Indians not members of any state, and to erect courts of final appeal to settle disputes between states over boundaries and other matters. To exercise most of the significant powers, a vote of nine states was required, while lesser matters could be settled by a majority.

The Articles of Confederation thus provided the basis

for the development of a more powerful central government. Congress lacked only the power to regulate trade and to raise money independent of requisitions upon the states, and within a few years it came close to achieving both. The great political mistake made by the supporters of this strictly federal government was that any changes in it had to be approved by all the states. Had the Articles of Confederation been easier to amend, it would have been far more difficult to replace in 1787-1788.

— 5 —

THE IDEA OF A NATIONAL GOVERNMENT

The Political Result of the Revolution.   The overriding constitutional and political result of the American Revolution, both in theory and governmental structure, was an enormous increase in the democratic potential:

(1) After 1776 the majority of voters in each state, if agreed upon a program, could put it into effect without any of the internal or external checks provided by British appointed governors, upper houses, and judiciaries, and in the last resort, by the British government in London.

(2) The revolution in theory was absolute, for governments deriving their authority from above were replaced by governments based on the sovereignty of the people, and that idea, however much thwarted in practice, was a potent force that could never again be ignored.

(3) The power of a sovereign central government was replaced by a strictly federal government controlled by the states.

(4) The hierarchy of state officials, most of whom had been appointed before 1776, was replaced by officials who, directly or indirectly, owed their positions to the will of the voters.

(5) The idea that a man was entitled to vote and to

hold office because he was a man, and not because he owned a certain amount of property or had a particular religion, made its appearance, and a beginning was made to put it into effect, as was the idea that representation should be according to population and not according to area or to wealth.

After 1776 the sovereign and independent states set about regulating commerce, adopting protective tariffs, encouraging industry, and altering the patterns of taxation. After the war, when a scarcity of money made it difficult for the farmers to pay their private debts and the heavy taxes levied to pay war debts, 7 of the 13 states issued paper money and passed legislation to delay foreclosures on farm mortgages. Paper money, which had been abandoned before the end of the war, was now bitterly opposed by merchants, wealthy planters, and creditors, but the pressure of the farmers, who were the vast majority of the population, was too powerful to be resisted. And when farmers could not get what they wanted from their legislators, they could threaten to use force, as they did in Massachusetts in 1786-1787.

The Opposition to Democracy. Whatever posterity may think, many important leaders in the eighteenth century did not in fact believe that the majority of ordinary men could govern themselves without restraint. They were convinced that democracy had come to America as a result of the American Revolution, and they believed that its coming was evil. They had feared such a result before the Declaration of Independence, and the events in the states during and after the war confirmed their fears. The times were not as bad as some American leaders pictured them, but their dislike of what had happened—and even more, their fear of what might happen—was a real and powerful political force. Hence they worked unceasingly to change the governments created during the revolutionary upheaval. To say this is not to assert that the Founding Fathers were engaged in a "conspiracy," as some naïve writers have charged. Even the slightest acquaintance with the sources reveals that many eighteenth-century leaders did not believe in democracy, either in theory or in practice, and they made no secret of it. They denounced it in private letters, but also in the newspapers, in pamphlets, and in poetry. Furthermore, it should be remembered that in the eighteenth century it was still possible to denounce democracy in public and yet win elections.

Many a colonial leader, as he became a citizen of the new states, scorned the "new men" who rose to power and the "lower orders" who followed them. Thus, Gouverneur Morris in New York decried the "herd of mechanicks" who got military commissions while the gentry were often ignored. Samuel Johnston of North Carolina was shocked because gentlemen were no longer treated with respect. In 1782 a Massachusetts merchant, alarmed at the insecurity of property, wondered who would not fly "to any refuge from anarchy and plebeian despotism?" Jeremy Belknap, a New England clergyman, commented in 1784 that "democratic government" was "to say the least . . . extremely inconvenient." In the same year a South Carolina planter wailed that "gentlemen of property" too often lost elections to the "lower classes." After Shays's Rebellion broke out in Massachusetts, Noah Webster, in a widely reprinted newspaper article, announced that he would "definitely prefer a limited monarchy," for he would rather be subject to the "caprice of one man than to the ignorance of a multitude." In 1787 General Henry Knox declared that "a mad democracy sweeps away every moral and divine trait from human character. Hence it is that reason, law, and patriotism is banished from almost every legislature." Perhaps no one summed up the prevailing attitude of the more extreme opponents of democracy better than an army officer who wrote in 1788 that "the philosophy that teaches the equality of mankind and the dignity of human nature is founded in vanity and addressed to it alone . . . there is infinitely more truth in the opposite doctrine that the many were made for the few, and that we are better governed by rods than by reason."

The Demand for a Strong Central Government. The men who deplored what they thought were the democratic results of the Revolution sought to retain control of the state governments, and in some states they were fairly successful. But such control was uncertain at best because of annual elections and legislative supremacy. The other thing they could do (and many of them tried to do it continuously from the beginning of the war) was to create a central government powerful enough to regulate and limit the actions of the states and their citizens. Such men argued that a powerful central government was needed to regulate trade, to control the amount and value of money issued, to suppress rebellions within states, to win the war, to pay the war debts, and the like.

They failed when the Articles of Confederation were written, but as soon as the Articles were ratified, three outstanding and consistent believers in a strong central government—James Madison, James Duane, and James Varnum—were appointed by Congress to propose measures for putting the Confederation into effect. They at once suggested that Congress be given power to impress property in wartime, to appoint tax collectors, and to seize the property of delinquent states. Congress ignored these proposals, which were so contrary to the spirit and the text of the constitution. During the same year Congress proposed an amendment to the Confederation giving it the power to levy import duties. Because of the wartime need for money, 12 states soon approved, but Rhode Island refused the necessary unanimous consent on the grounds that it would alter the character of the central government and endanger liberty. When Virginia joined Rhode Island by repealing her own act of approval, the amendment was killed.

Between 1781 and 1783 Congress was controlled by men who wanted a strong central government, and they argued that the war could not be won without it. But by 1783 the war was won, and in desperation some of them plotted a *coup d'état*. Men like Robert Morris, Gouverneur Morris, and Alexander Hamilton hoped to unite the discontented army officers and the public creditors, and they had the help of generals Henry Knox, Alexander McDougall, Horatio Gates, and lesser army officers. The scheme was for the army to refuse to fight if the war did not end and to refuse to disband if it did. All depended on Washington's leadership, but he killed the scheme in a speech at Newburgh on the Hudson in March 1783.

His action was a striking reversal of what many believed was a lesson of history: that at the end of a successful war the military hero of the war usually took over the government by force and became a dictator in fact if not in name. What Washington's action meant, so far as he and the country were concerned, was that political change must be brought about by political means and not by armed force. His contemporaries, who, unlike posterity, knew their history, knew what they meant when they called him the "American Cincinnatus."

At war's end, defeated at every turn, the proponents of a strong central government continued to try to acquire more power for Congress. Once more they tried to give it the power to collect import duties, and they campaigned hard to give it the power to regulate trade. By 1786 all the states except New York had granted the power to collect duties, and even New York gave a qualified permission, but the power to regulate trade was defeated by the southern planters. They were convinced that this power would result in a monopoly of shipping for the northern merchants, and hence higher freight rates for southern exports, and they would have none of it.

Opposition to a stronger central government had deeper roots. Robert Morris, as superintendent of finance from 1781 to 1784, had dominated Congress and was the acknowledged leader of those who wanted what was coming to be called a "national government." He had been openly contemptuous of opposition and impatient with constitutional restraints and procedures. His financial program was widely believed to be directed toward enriching himself and his friends at the expense of the country. His methods, his attitudes, and his program, which anticipated the Federalist program, even to details, alienated even men who sympathized with his ultimate goals. More importantly, he alarmed those revolutionary leaders who clung to the political ideals of 1776. By the 1780's most of them were agreed that the central government must have more power, but they were afraid that men like Morris would undo the basic political and constitutional achievements of the Revolution if they were not blocked. As Richard Henry Lee put it, those who demanded more power for Congress would not rest "until every fence is thrown down that was designed to protect and cover the rights of mankind." And he repeated once more the doctrine that "power poisons the mind of its possessor and aids him to remove the shackles that restrain itself."

The Origins of the Philadelphia Convention. Faced with opposition at every level, the nationalists eventually gave up the attempt to change the Articles of Confederation by either amendment or interpretation. More and more they turned to the idea of a convention which might by-pass the constitutional procedure for amending the federal constitution: proposal of amendments by Congress and unanimous ratification by the 13 states. In so doing the nationalists were adopting the methods of the revolutionary leaders who had used extra-legal and extra-constitutional bodies to achieve independence.

From 1780 onward there were proposals for conventions almost every year in private letters, newspapers, and state legislatures. Thus, in 1780 Hamilton suggested a convention to create a powerful central government and to adopt one without reference to Congress, the legislatures, or the people, and to use the army to put it into effect if need be. In 1783 Washington sent a circular letter to the states appealing for more power for the central government. It was hoped that the appeal would bring about a convention, but it had no effect. In 1785 the Massachusetts legislature directed its delegates in Congress to propose a convention, but they refused on the grounds that a convention would be used by a group of men in the United States to destroy the political fabric created by the Articles of Confederation.

In January 1786, on the urging of James Madison and his allies, the Virginia legislature took the step that was at last to lead to a convention. Virginia invited the states to send delegates to Annapolis, Maryland, in September to discuss matters relating to the regulation of commerce. This call from Virginia aroused suspicion among merchants, since Virginia had consistently refused to grant Congress the power to regulate trade. And when the merchants learned the names of the delegates, they suspected that "political objects" were involved. Among the delegates were James Madison, Alexander Hamilton, and John Dickinson, none of whom were involved in commerce, but who had been outspoken in their demands for a strong central government.

The Annapolis Convention met on September 11 and disbanded on September 14, 1786. Its report, submitted to Congress and the states, declared that the power of regulating trade could not be given to the federal government without adjustments in other parts of the federal system. It therefore suggested that a convention meet in Philadelphia the following spring to devise further provisions to "render the constitution of the federal government adequate to the exigencies of the union. . . ." The French consul in New York, in sending a translation to his government, commented that the report contained "an infinity of circumlocutions and ambiguous phrases" to hide the purpose of the convention from the people at large. The people, he observed, had resisted every attempt to increase the strength of the central government. Now, because of commercial difficulties, the people might agree to a change, not realizing what plans their leaders had in mind. The more enlightened citizens, he said, such as "gentlemen" and merchants, would not fail to seize the opportunity offered.

Whether he was right or wrong, there was little public reaction. In fact, a number of men like John Jay, who wanted to strengthen the government, believed that a convention was not the proper way: the United States had a constitution, and its procedures should be followed. When Congress met in the fall of 1786, the Massachusetts delegation insisted that Congress should not call a convention, but itself propose amendments to be sent to the states. Congress took no action on the report of the Annapolis Convention, but Virginia, Pennsylvania, and New Jersey elected delegates to a convention anyway. The rest of the states rejected the report of the Annapolis Convention or ignored it as Congress had done.

But a storm was breaking in Massachusetts in the fall of 1786 which alarmed many leaders from one end of America to the other and changed the minds of those in Massachusetts. Shays's Rebellion was an uprising of the backcountry farmers against the taxation policies of Massachusetts and the rigorous action of the courts in foreclosing farm mortgages and jailing men for debt. The farmers closed the courts and then took up arms to protect themselves. The state government borrowed money, hired troops, sent them west, and the rebellion vanished. It was over by February 1787, but its impact was not.

When Congress met again in January 1787, the question was whether it would call a convention. Many men in and out of Congress felt that a convention would not be legal unless Congress did call it, and some doubted the legality even if it did so. Congress delayed a decision, but by mid-February all of the southern states had elected delegates, and it was well known that Washington would head the Virginia delegation. At last, on February 21, Congress agreed to call a convention to meet in Philadelphia in May for

> the sole and express purpose of revising the Articles of Confederation and reporting to Congress and the several legislatures such alterations and provisions therein, as shall, when agreed to in Congress and confirmed by the states, render the federal constitution adequate to the exigencies of government and the preservation of the union.

Officially, then, Congress called the convention to revise the Articles of Confederation, with the revisions to be considered and approved or rejected in the manner prescribed by that document. If the members of Congress were aware that a political revolution lay ahead, they did not acknowledge it. But such a revolution was already under way: in the structure of the central government, in the balance of power between it and the states, and in the means by which the new government was to be established.

— 6 —

THE BEGINNINGS OF THE CONVENTION OF 1787

Plans for a New Constitution.   The Constitutional Convention met at the end of May 1787, but preparations for it began months before. During the winter of 1786-1787 the men who did more than any others to shape the outcome of the Convention were making plans for a new government and for securing its ratification. By the time the Convention was organized, the broad principles upon which it was to proceed had been agreed upon. The nationalist leaders had no intention of merely revising the Articles of Confederation. They wanted to create a government free from subordination to and control by the state legislatures; one which, in contrast, would have the power to control both the states and their citizens. Furthermore, they proposed to abandon the internal structure of the existing government. The single-house Congress under the Confederation was essentially a parliamentary body exercising executive and judicial as well as legislative power. The executive officers of the government—the secretaries of foreign affairs and war, and the committee in charge of the treasury—were elected by Congress, responsible to it, and removable at any time. The president was merely a presiding officer who was elected annually.

The men who planned the Convention were convinced that this "parliamentary" Congress must be replaced by a "balanced" government consisting of separate legislative, judicial, and executive departments, each independent and acting as a check upon the others. Their ideas were revealed, among other places, in the letters Washington received in answer to his requests for opinions about what form the new government should take. John Jay, who as secretary for foreign affairs had been badly bruised by Congress, replied that it should not be given more power. Congress should retain legislative power, but there should be a separate executive and judiciary. As for structure, Jay suggested that Congress should be divided into an annually elected lower house and an upper house appointed for life. He was opposed to a monarchy, but he wanted an executive who, with a council of judges, would have the power to veto acts of Congress. In any event, the country must have a government suited to "our manners and circumstances" which "are not strictly democratical." As for the states, they should retain power only for domestic purposes and all their civil and military officers should be appointed and removed by "the national government."

General Henry Knox, the secretary of war, who had done much to arouse alarm by his descriptions of the Shaysites in Massachusetts as "levellers" bent upon dividing up the property of the rich, told Washington that there should be a lower house, an upper house, and an executive chosen by them to serve during good behavior. As for power, the laws of the central government must be obeyed by the states, and if necessary, "enforced by a body of armed men to be kept for the purpose. . . ."

Knox's ideas were those of a body of extremists whose main aim was to establish control over hitherto unchecked state legislative majorities which were, to them, examples of democracy run rampant. After the Convention met, he wrote to one of its members: "the state systems are the accursed thing which will prevent our being a nation . . . the vile state governments are sources of pollution which will contaminate the American name for ages . . . smite them in the name of God and the people."

James Madison agreed that the states must be put under the control of the central government. The principal means, which he argued for before, during, and after the Convention, was the veto of state legislation by Congress. When Edmund Randolph proposed that the Convention should retain the structure of the Articles of Confederation, Madison replied that the independence of the states was "utterly irreconcilable with the idea of an aggregate sovereignty." Representation should be by population and not by states, and any new constitution must be ratified by the people and not by the state legislatures. As for the central government, it too must be radically changed by dividing it into separate and independent departments, each with a check upon the others. However, he refused to go along with the extremists who wanted to abolish the states and set up a single republic. He hoped to find some "middle ground" which would support a supreme "national authority" while leaving in force the "local authorities so far as they can be subordinately useful."

Before the Convention met, then, it is clear that there was agreement among the nationalists upon certain broad principles:

(1) that the federal government must be replaced by a national government with power to control the states and their citizens; in other words, that effective sovereignty must be transferred from the states to the central government;

(2) that the single-house Congress of the Articles of Confederation must be replaced by a three-branch government, each branch independent of and acting as a check upon the others;

(3) that the old principle of equality of the states must be replaced by representation according to population in both houses of the new Congress.

While the broad principles were clear, the nationalists differed among themselves as to means of achieving their ends, and they were to meet with strong opposition from those in the Convention who insisted upon retaining at least a portion of the old federal structure in the new government. Old quarrels, too, such as those between the large and the small and between the northern and the southern states, were to divide the Convention, and they had to be compromised. But the nationalist leaders never lost sight of the ultimate goal of creating a more powerful central government, and they achieved a measure of what they intended, although not as much as many of them hoped for.

The Convention Begins.   All of the state legislatures except Rhode Island elected delegates. Of the 74 men chosen, 55 appeared in the Convention—although some came late, as did the New Hampshire delegation, which did not arrive until the end of July, and others left before the Convention was over, among them Robert Yates and John Lansing of New York and Luther Martin of Maryland. Of the 55 men who attended, not more than a dozen were the key figures in the Convention and in writing the Constitution. The great majority merely voted and kept silent. Of the dozen, James Madison, James Wilson, and Gouverneur Morris were the outstanding nationalist leaders. In the middle were such men as George Mason, John Dickinson, Oliver Ellsworth, and John Rutledge, who supported the idea of a strong central government, but who insisted on an important role for the states in the new system. Among those who wished to retain the federal structure of the old government, although believing it should be strengthened, were Roger Sherman, William Paterson, Elbridge Gerry, and Luther Martin, the last being the most vocal opponent of the Constitution in its final form. Alexander Hamilton of New York was present part of the time, but Yates and Lansing consistently cast the ballot of that state against everything Hamilton stood for as long as they were in the Convention. Perhaps the most important single member of the Convention, although he voted only a few times and spoke only once for the record, was George Washington. His presence, as his friends said, gave the Convention a "national complexion," and his support of the Constitution probably did more to secure its ratification than the hundreds of speeches and newspaper articles of men of lesser reputation.

The Convention was called to meet on May 14, but a quorum of seven states was not present until May 25, when Washington was unanimously elected president. On Monday and Tuesday of the next week the Convention adopted rules. It was agreed that each state should have one vote, to be determined by the majority of each delegation, and when a delegation was equally divided its vote would not count. In this the Convention followed the rules of Congress, although before the Convention opened the Pennsylvania delegates had proposed that the large states unite to deny the small states equality. The Virginia delegation "discountenanced and stifled the project," not wanting a head-on struggle which might wreck the Convention at the outset. A second rule was for the Convention to meet in secret, a decision that was to meet with bitter criticism once the Constitution was published. A third and most important rule was that no vote was to be taken as final, thus allowing questions to be reopened for discussion and a new vote as members changed their minds.

With the adoption of rules the Convention was ready to begin, and the Virginia delegation was ready with a program. The Virginians had arrived early and had held regular meetings in which they had prepared a set of resolutions as a basis for discussion. (*See Reading No. 1.*) These were presented to the Convention by Governor Edmund Randolph, who, as he was soon to show, did not agree with all of them.

A National Government the Remedy for Democracy. Randolph opened the formal proceedings on May 29 with a speech declaring that the central government should have the power to defend itself and the country and that it should be "paramount to the state constitutions." He expressed high regard for the authors of the Articles of Confederation, but said that "human rights were the chief knowledge of the times when it was framed so far as they applied to oppose Great Britain." Under the Articles Congress could not prevent war or support one. The states might provoke war and there was no way to control them. The federal government had no power to suppress quarrels among states nor to suppress rebellion in any one of them. When the Articles were written there was no commercial discord among states, rebellion had not appeared in Massachusetts, foreign debts were not urgent, the havoc of paper money had not been foreseen, and treaties had not been violated.

Randolph concluded by asserting that the "chief danger arises from the democratic parts of our constitutions. It is a maxim which I hold incontrovertible that the powers of government exercised by the people swallows up the other branches. None of the [*state*] constitutions have provided sufficient checks against the democracy." Two days later, in speaking of the proposed senate, he commented that its purpose was to provide a cure for the evils of the United States, and that in "tracing these evils to their origin every man had found it in the turbulence and follies of democracy. . . ." No one, either then or later in the Convention, disagreed with this analysis. In fact, this assumption was so commonly accepted that while the members mentioned it repeatedly during the Convention, they found no need to discuss it at length.

The specific expression of "democracy" in the states, about which the Convention was so much concerned, was primarily economic legislation. By the end of 1786 many states had adopted laws suspending or delaying the collection of debts and taxes, seven of them had once again issued paper money, and there was a powerful demand for paper money in the remainder. Early in the Convention Madison stated that it was the fear of such legislation that did more to bring about the Convention than any other factor.

The remedy for the evils of democracy—of unchecked state legislative majorities—was the replacement of the existing federal government by a national government. In presenting 15 resolutions to the Convention on May 29, Randolph "candidly confessed that they were not intended for a federal government. He meant a strong consolidated union in which the idea of states should be nearly annihilated." Madison reported the statement a little differently than Yates of New York: "He pointed out the various defects of the federal system, the necessity of transforming it into a national, efficient government. . . ."

However, the first of the Virginia resolutions called for correction and enlargement of the Articles of Confederation. Gouverneur Morris pointed out at once that this was contradicted by the remaining 14 resolutions. Randolph therefore withdrew it and offered three others that were to the point: (1) that a merely federal union would not accomplish the purposes of the Articles of Confederation; (2) that no treaty among sovereign states could achieve their common defense, liberty, or welfare; (3) that "a national government ought to be established consisting of a supreme judicial, legislative, and executive."

These resolutions presented the Convention with a fundamental decision. It had been called to revise and amend the Articles of Confederation, and it was now proposed to abandon them. General Charles C. Pinckney* of South Carolina at once told the delegates that if they declared the federal government inadequate, the Convention was at an end because it had no power to make such a declaration. The Convention at first evaded the issue by dropping the first two resolutions, but 33 of the 55 men were lawyers accustomed to interpreting the meaning of words. What did the word "supreme" mean in the third resolution, asked one of them? Gouverneur Morris placed the issue squarely before the Convention when he "explained the distinction between a federal and [a] national, supreme, government; the former being a mere compact resting on the good faith of the parties; the latter having a complete and compulsive operation."

Elbridge Gerry then suggested that a distinction between a national and a federal government should not be made because it was doubtful that the Convention had the authority to propose a totally different government from the existing one, or that Congress would have the right to agree to one. Why not resolve to create a "federal" legislature, executive, and judiciary instead? The Convention ignored him and resolved that "a national government ought to be established consisting of a supreme legislative, judiciary, and executive."

As opposition to the nationalist program grew, and as

---

* C. C. Pinckney will be referred to as General Pinckney, to distinguish him from Charles Pinckney.

the nationalist leaders came to realize that the substance of power was more important than its labels, they agreed to drop the word "national" wherever it appeared. But they never wavered in their basic aim of creating a national government, supreme over the states, however much they had to yield to opposition and political realities.

— 7 —

NATIONALISM VS. FEDERALISM: THE VIRGINIA AND THE NEW JERSEY PLANS

The Virginia Plan. The Virginia resolutions proposed a revolutionary shift in power from the states to the central government and a radical revision in the internal structure of the central government itself. There would be a two-house congress* with voting in each house according to the free inhabitants of each state (or contributions by the states to common expenses). The new congress, unlike the old one, would be freed from state control, for the house of representatives would be elected by the voters of the states, not by the state legislatures. The only role left to the latter would be the nomination of senators to be elected by the national house of representatives. The national congress would have all the powers of Congress under the Articles of Confederation. In addition, it would have the power to subject the states entirely to its will. It would legislate where the states were "incompetent" or the "harmony" of the United States might be interrupted by the individual states. It would veto state legislation which in its opinion violated the national con-

---

* In this account the names finally agreed upon by the Convention have been used: congress, president, senate, and house (for house of representatives).

stitution, and use force against any state not doing its duty. All state governors, judges, and legislators would be required to take an oath to support the "articles of union."

The central government itself would be dominated by congress, and the very center of power would be the house of representatives, which would choose the senate. The two houses together would elect an executive, who would be ineligible for a second term, and the judges of the national courts, who would serve during good behavior. The national executive would have the authority to execute the acts of congress and possess the executive powers of Congress under the Articles of Confederation. Acting with a council of national judges, the executive would have the power to veto acts of congress, including those vetoing state legislation, but such vetoes could be overridden by congress. The national judiciary would consist of one or more supreme courts and of inferior courts. The national courts would hear cases involving piracies and felonies on the high seas, cases in which foreigners and citizens of different states were interested, cases concerning the collection of national revenue, impeachments of national officers, and cases concerning the national peace and harmony.

The proposed government, after approval by the old Congress, would not be submitted to the state legislatures for ratification, as under the Articles of Confederation, but to state conventions "expressly chosen by the people, to consider and decide thereon."

The Convention went into a committee of the whole, and for the next two weeks it debated the resolutions presented by Edmund Randolph. During those debates most of the basic ideas and issues that occupied the delegates until September became perfectly clear. In fact, in many areas, nothing essentially new was said after the first two weeks. The division between those who wanted to create a national government and those who wanted to add more powers to the existing federal government was apparent from the start. So, too, was the conflict between the large states and the small states over voting in congress. The rival views of the northern and southern states appeared, but did not become important until later. Nationalist leaders such as Madison and Wilson soon showed that they had no more trust in a powerful national legislature than they had in the state legislatures. Men who agreed on ultimate goals differed as to the means of achieving them, and they tended to reflect the interests of their states and their sections when those seemed in conflict with such goals. Men were to change their minds and their votes during the course of the Convention, but the arguments they used were often repetitious.

Debate on the Virginia Plan. The Virginia resolutions were debated in order, but some of them were turned to again and again before the committee of the whole delivered a report upon those resolutions on June 13. It is, therefore, necessary to discuss them topically to achieve a measure of clarity.

The proposal to destroy the equality of the states in congress by substituting representation according to population or contributions at once raised an issue that embittered and for a time threatened the existence of the Convention. The nationalist leaders insisted that proportional representation was the indispensable foundation for a national government, and to justify it they adopted the revolutionary principle of the sovereignty of the people. The sovereign people, they argued, had delegated one portion of their authority to the state governments. Now they were to be asked to delegate another portion of it to a national government. The adoption of the theoretical foundation of the Revolution is evidence of the political genius of the nationalist leaders, but it does not mean that they subscribed to its practical implications.

They hoped that a national government, based on the sovereignty of the people, would limit that sovereignty as a political fact. A national government would first of all check the state legislatures in which, they believed, democracy was demonstrating its evils. Furthermore, representation by population and the election of at least the house of representatives by the people would eliminate the control of the state legislatures over the central government. Then, too, the adoption of the theory of popular sovereignty would justify ignoring the constitutional procedure of the Articles of Confederation: proposal of amendments by Congress and unanimous ratification by the state legislatures. It would justify, too, the action of the Convention in ignoring the call of Congress to revise the Articles and in appealing directly to the people for ratification.

But the demand for proportional representation had another purpose, and that was to secure more votes for the largest states. Most of the members of the Convention agreed that the central government should have more power, but on the issue of equality for the states, as opposed to proportional representation, some of them were ready to fight, and the nationalist leaders were in a weak position. The more important among them—James Madison, James Wilson, Gouverneur Morris, and Rufus King —were from the three largest states. Virginia alone had 20 per cent, and Virginia, Pennsylvania, and Massachusetts combined had close to half the total population of the United States. However much they might disagree on other issues, representatives of those states were united in resentment at the equality of the small states. Ever since Patrick Henry had declared in the First Continental Congress that he was an American, not a Virginian, in a vain effort to secure more votes for Virginia, the large states had wanted representation according to population.

Intellectually, men like Madison and Wilson might transcend state lines, but emotionally they could not escape the fact that they represented states with a grievance. In unguarded moments, and sometimes in anger, they revealed that fact, and their opponents were not slow to seize upon such revelations and to point out that high principle and lesser motives were at odds, that behind principle lay a desire of the three great states to dominate the United States. Whatever the validity of such fears, they were a political fact of the times which dictated the actions of men in the Convention, as they had those of men since 1774 and were to continue to do after 1787. When the issue was first presented to the Convention, Read threatened that the Delaware delegation would walk out, since its instructions forbade it to surrender the equality of the states. In reply Gouverneur Morris asserted that proportional representation was "so fundamental an article in a national government that it could not be dispensed with," and Madison added that equality must be abandoned when a federal union among sovereign states was replaced by a national government. However, the Convention agreed to postpone discussion in the vain hope that in the end only Delaware would object to proportional representation.

The Convention then turned to the proposal for popular election of the house of representatives. Opposition to it came from two sources: from those who wanted to retain the federal government, and from some of the men alarmed at the popular excesses of the times. As Roger Sherman saw it, the issue was simply one of whether or not the state governments should be abolished, and he proposed election of the house by the state legislatures. The objects of the central government were few, he said, and all the rest should be left to the states. Throughout the Convention he worked for an important role for the states. On the other hand, Elbridge Gerry, hag-ridden by the memory of Shays's Rebellion, talked of the evils of democracy and opposed popular elections. He was joined by the South Carolina delegates who were for a national government, but who did not think that the voters should have any direct influence upon it.

James Wilson was the most vigorous supporter of popular elections, not because he believed in democracy in practice, but because popular elections would free the central government from state control. As he explained it, he was for "raising the federal pyramid to a considerable altitude" and therefore giving it "as broad a basis as possible." Popular elections would give the people that confidence in the government which is so necessary in a republic. Madison's argument was more philosophical in that he said "popular election of one branch of the national legislature" was "essential to every plan of free government." But to those who feared too great popular influence, he had a practical answer. He was for "refining the popular appointments by successive filtrations" and said it would be safe to have popular election of the house if such "filtrations" were applied to the senate, the judiciary, and the executive, which would be beyond any direct popular control.

Support for popular election came from others. George Mason, one of Virginia's most respected leaders, made his only appearance on the national scene at the Convention. He said that the democratic principle must be represented in any balanced government and that the house of representatives should be the "grand depository of the democratic principle of the government." He agreed that "we" had become too democratic, but that there was danger in running to the opposite extreme. The rights of every class must be considered, and he wondered at the indifference of the "superior classes" to the "lowest classes of society" to which their posterity would inevitably belong.

Popular election of the house was voted six states to two, with two states divided, but the question was taken up again a few days later when Charles Pinckney moved, as Sherman had done, that the state legislatures elect the house. He said they would be better judges than the people and less likely to oppose the new government. George Mason agreed that much of what was said against democratic elections was true, but said that he believed with Wilson that large election districts would avoid much of the danger.

It was upon this occasion that Madison outlined in a long speech his conception of the purpose of the Convention and presented the essential argument that he was to use again in the Convention and was to express in final form in the tenth *Federalist.* The national government must provide security for private rights and steady dispensation of justice, and it was interference with these, more than anything else, that had produced the Convention. The solution was "to enlarge the sphere as far as the nature of the government would admit. This was the only defense against the inconveniences of democracy consistent with the democratic form of government." All societies are divided into many sects, factions, and interests, and whenever a majority are united in "a common interest or passion, the rights of the minority are in danger." Honesty, respect for character, conscience, and religion were all incapable of restraining such majorities, as all history proved, including the history of the United States since 1776. The thing to do, said Madison, was to so "enlarge the sphere" as to divide the community into such a number of interests and parties that they could never unite at any one time. Madison believed that if a "republican" government, as contrasted with the "democratic" state governments, were extended over the whole of the United States, the widely scattered interests would never be able to unite and get control of it. And even if they did get control of the house, then the senate, executive, and judiciary would still provide adequate protection for minorities.

The renewed debate had no effect. On June 6 the Convention settled finally that the house of representatives should be elected by popular vote. But the nationalists met defeat when it came to the senate. On the following day the defenders of the states went into action. The Convention rejected election of the senate by the house from nominations by state legislatures and ignored Wilson's suggestion that it be elected by the people. John Dickinson proposed that the senate be elected by the state legislatures, and many supported him. Wilson and Madison carried the whole argument for the nationalists, but they could make no headway against those who believed with Dickinson that the preservation of the states was indispensable and that any attempt to abolish them or limit them too sharply would be ruinous. The Convention voted ten states to none that the state legislatures should elect the senate.

The same issue of the relationship between the central government and the states was raised again in the debate over the sweeping grant of powers to Congress. Some delegates thought that those powers should be enumerated, but they were borne down, and there was no recorded objection to giving Congress the power to veto state laws violating the Constitution. In fact, the Convention added without argument Franklin's proposal that Congress have the right to veto state laws in conflict with national treaties. However, the proposal that Congress use force against the states was set aside after Madison said that a system ought to be evolved which would make the use of force unnecessary.

The gains of the nationalists were partly undone on June 8 by their overeagerness. The defenders of the states were consolidating their forces as they showed the day before in voting that the state legislatures should elect the senate. Not satisfied with the wide veto power given Congress, Charles Pinckney moved that Congress have the power to veto all state laws it thought improper, arguing that such a "universality of the power" was needed for an effective national government. Madison agreed that "an indefinite power to negative" state legislation was "absolutely necessary to a perfect system," and James Wilson backed him up. Spokesmen for the small states fought back. Bedford of Delaware saw in the proposal nothing but a plot of Pennsylvania and Virginia to create a system "in which they would have an enormous and monstrous influence." Some color was given to the charge when only Virginia, Pennsylvania, and Massachusetts voted for the absolute veto while the other seven states voted against it.

The debates on the president and the courts produced some of the same divisions, but revealed still other facets of political opinion. Edmund Randolph led those who supported a plural executive and who believed that a single president would be too much like an elective monarch. But this issue was settled once and for all on June 4 when the Convention voted seven to three for a single executive. Only New York, Maryland, and Delaware opposed, while the tie vote in the Virginia delegation was broken by one of Washington's rare votes.

Far more difficult was the question of how to elect the president, a matter that was to be the subject of much debate in the months ahead. The nationalists were opposed to election by the legislature because they wanted an independent and powerful executive, but they were not sure how else it could be done. James Wilson proposed election by the people to avoid intervention by the states, but he got no support. He next proposed what amounted to an "electoral college" whereby the people of the states would be divided into districts which would elect electors who would in turn elect a president. Those who clung to the revolutionary ideal of an all-powerful legislature, as did Roger Sherman, insisted on election by Congress. Since the nationalists had no acceptable alternative at the moment, the Convention agreed eight to two that Congress would elect the president for a term of seven years.

The extent of the president's power excited far more debate. The Virginia plan proposed that he execute the laws of Congress, possess the executive powers of the old Congress, and with a council of judges, veto legislation of Congress, although the vetoes could be overridden. The right to exercise the executive powers of the old Congress was dropped at once because those involved the power of making peace and war. There was even stronger objection to associating judges in the use of the veto power. As Elbridge Gerry put it, the judges had enough protection since the exposition of the laws "involved a power of deciding on their constitutionality." The veto power itself came under heavy attack, the extreme opinion on one side being that there should be no check at all on legislative action. This attitude, of course, reflected the provisions of all but one of the state constitutions. George Mason, who was opposed to a single executive, saw in the veto power the threat of the most dangerous kind of monarchy, "an elective one." Despite all the oppressions and injustices "experienced among us from democracy," the genius of the people was for it and they must be consulted, and Madison agreed that the absolute veto would be obnoxious in the present temper of the country. The extreme nationalist opinion was expressed by Wilson and Hamilton, who moved that the president should have an absolute veto as the only means to make him independent, but their argument that it would not be used convinced no one. Their motion was rejected unanimously. The Convention then agreed that the president alone should have the veto power, but that it could be overridden by a two-thirds vote of each house.

The discussion of the judiciary began a controversy that was to entangle American politics for years to come, as in the struggle over the judiciary acts of 1789 and 1801. The Convention decided that there should be but one supreme court, but the nationalists opposed election by Congress. Wilson insisted that there would be too much intrigue and argued for appointment by the president. The counter argument was that this would give too much power to one man. Madison was in between: he was for appointment by the senate and this was agreed to.

But the big issue was that of inferior courts. John Rutledge, Chief Justice of South Carolina, argued that there should be none, that the state courts should handle all cases in the first instance, leaving an appeal open to the national supreme court, and he was supported by defenders of state power such as Sherman of Connecticut. Inferior courts, like a supreme court, were one of the key parts of the nationalist program. As Madison put it, "an effective judiciary establishment commensurate to the legislative authority was essential." Rutledge's motion lost by the narrow margin of five to four, with two states divided. The Virginia plan made it mandatory that Congress establish inferior courts; Wilson and Madison moved that the power be discretionary. The concession failed to satisfy Connecticut and South Carolina, but it did eight states, and in its final form the Constitution gave Congress discretionary power.

Lesser parts of the Virginia plan were agreed to rapidly, although there were some close votes. The requirement that state officers take an oath to support the Constitution passed six to five. A three-year term for the house and a seven-year term for the senate were agreed to after sharp division of opinion. Several members wanted a three-year term for the senate, but seven years was agreed to after Randolph asserted that the "democratic licentiousness" of the state legislatures proved the need for a "firm senate" and that the object of the senate was to "control the democratic branch of the national legislature." The plan for ratification by state conventions, which had been worked out before the Convention met, was the subject of considerable debate. Men like Sherman insisted that the Articles of Confederation provided the way, while those alarmed by popular excesses, such as Gerry, opposed any reference to the people. Ratification by "the people" was essential to the nationalist plan on both theoretical and practical grounds: theoretical because it was the justification for creating a national government, and practical because the nationalists were convinced that the state legislatures would never ratify. The vote for reference to state conventions was six to five, but the issue was to crop up again and again, although the decision made on June 12 was not to be changed.

During the debate on the Virginia resolutions two contrasting views became ever more clear. The extreme nationalists, such as James Madison, James Wilson, Alexander Hamilton, and Gouverneur Morris, wanted to subject the states absolutely to a national government. Their ideal, perhaps, was the abolition of the states, but at the very least they wanted to reduce them to mere administrative districts. The opposition came from a variety of men and for various reasons. The extreme federalists, such as Yates and Lansing of New York and Martin of Maryland, wanted to retain the federal structure intact although they agreed that the central government must have more power. In this they were supported by delegates from the small states such as Paterson of New Jersey and Read of Delaware, who also agreed that there was need for more centralized power, but who insisted that above all the states should retain their equality in at least one branch of the legislature. Read, for instance, was a nationalist once he had won that point. The largest and most important group—John Dickinson, George Mason, Oliver Ellsworth, Roger Sherman, Edmund Randolph, and others—were likewise supporters of greater central power, but they insisted that at least a portion of the old federal structure must be retained in the new government. With them it was a matter of deep political conviction and a question of sheer political necessity. Unlike such foreign-born delegates as Hamilton, Wilson, and Robert Morris, these men had an understanding of and a feeling for the hold of the states on the minds of Americans.

The issue of the relation of the central government to the states was implicit or explicit in every vote taken, but the big fight centered around proportional representation. It had been dropped on May 30 when Delaware threatened to walk out, but Paterson of New Jersey put it squarely before the Convention on June 9 when he made a frontal assault on the whole nationalist position. He moved that the Convention resume discussion of representation and pointed out that it was an old dispute which had been settled rightly, so far as he was concerned, in the Articles of Confederation. Proportional representation threatened the existence of the smaller states and would give all power to the three largest. Paterson challenged the legality of the Convention if it agreed to the Virginia plan, for "the idea of a national government as contradistinguished from a federal one" had not been in the minds of the states when they elected and instructed delegates. The Articles of Confederation should be amended to define the powers of the states and give Congress the power of coercion "which was the great point." James Wilson had hinted that the large states might confederate together; let them do so, but let them remember that they had no power to coerce others.

In the debate which followed many of the arguments were the same as those used during the writing of the Articles of Confederation in 1776 and 1777, and in some cases they were offered by the same men. James Wilson, Benjamin Franklin, and Roger Sherman repeated what they had said in 1776, while Paterson and Luther Martin used the arguments of John Witherspoon and Samuel Chase, who had represented New Jersey and Maryland eleven years before.

James Wilson argued as he had in 1776 that "all authority was derived from the people," but then he lost his temper at the thought of New Jersey's equality with Pennsylvania. "Shall New Jersey have the same right or influence in the councils of the nation with Pennsylvania? I say no. It is unjust. I will never confederate on this plan." It is little wonder that the smaller states thought in 1787, as they had in 1776, that the theoretical justification for proportional representation was a mere sham to disguise a plot by Virginia, Pennsylvania, and Massachusetts to get control of the United States. After Wilson's heated remarks Paterson suggested that they put off the debate until after the week end.

On Monday Roger Sherman offered the compromise which Dickinson had suggested earlier. He moved that voting in the house be by population and that each state have one vote in the senate. The states should be able to protect themselves in one branch, he said, or the large states would rule them all. The Convention agreed seven to three to another motion that voting in the house should be according to some equitable basis of representation. But what basis? Some wealthy South Carolina delegates thought that votes should be according to wealth, for "money was power," said one. However, most delegates would not support them. Wilson then made a suggestion which ultimately became part of the Constitution. Back in 1776 he had aroused the South Carolinians by attacking slaves as property, but now he held out political bait to them and other southern delegates who seemed to be wavering on representation according to population. He proposed that representation in the house be according to the number of free citizens of every age, sex, and condition, including indentured servants, and "three-fifths of all other persons" except Indians not paying taxes. The southerners had no objection at all to counting three-fifths of their slaves, and Charles Pinckney seconded the motion. Nine states voted for it and only Delaware and New Jersey opposed. This "political deal" was to haunt the nation, but it got the Convention over a hurdle, at least temporarily. A portent of what was to come within a few weeks was Elbridge Gerry's query as to why they should count slave property in the South any more than horses and cattle in the North.

Sherman then moved the next part of his compromise: that each state have one vote in the senate. It was turned down six states to five, the three large states plus the two Carolinas and Georgia against Connecticut, New York, New Jersey, Delaware, and Maryland. Wilson and Hamilton, for the triumphant nationalist large state-slave state combination, then moved that voting in the senate be according to population, and the Convention approved six to five. But within a month the large states were forced to yield on the senate to keep the Convention going.

The report on the Virginia resolutions was now complete, and it represented a triumph for the nationalists. (*See Reading No. 2.*) The Convention was now ready to vote formally on the 19 resolutions adopted by the "committee of the whole," but Paterson of New Jersey asked for a delay because several delegates wished to present a "purely federal" plan. The nationalists had gone too far and too fast. "You see," John Dickinson told Madison, "the consequence of pushing things too far." Several members from the smaller states were agreed on a two-branch legislature, he said, and were friendly to a national government, "but we would sooner submit to a foreign power than submit to be deprived of an equality of suffrage in both branches of the legislature, and thereby be thrown under the domination of the large states."

The fears of the small states were real, however exaggerated they may seem as one looks back. The Virginia plan provided for an all-powerful legislature, and if there were representation by population in both branches, the three large states would control Congress, and the presidency and the judiciary as well. Hence the delegates from the small states combined with those who believed in a truly federal government to offer the New Jersey plan to the Convention on June 15. Had it been offered at the beginning of the Convention it might well have been adopted.

The New Jersey Plan. The purpose of the New Jersey plan was to create a powerful central government by amending the Articles of Confederation, and in some respects the proposed amendments gave a more sweeping grant of power than did the final draft of the Constitution. But the government would remain strictly federal, and the states would retain their equality and their sovereignty in all matters not specifically delegated to Congress.

Congress would be given the power to levy imports, regulate trade, and collect funds from states not complying with congressional requisitions. There would be a federal supreme court with widespread powers. The acts of Congress and United States treaties would be "the supreme law of the respective states" and the state judiciaries would be bound by them, despite any state laws to the contrary. If a state or body of men within a state opposed or tried to prevent the execution of acts of Congress or treaties, the federal executive would be authorized to use force to compel obedience. (*See Reading No. 3.*)

As Lansing of New York put it, the two systems were "fairly contrasted." The New Jersey plan proposed to amend the constitution of the existing government, while the Virginia plan provided for a national government. One "sustains the sovereignty of the respective states" and the other "destroys it." Lansing argued that the Convention did not have the power to create a national government, and if one were proposed, it would be rejected. Paterson took the legal ground that the Articles of Confederation had been the unanimous creation of the states, and that if they were abandoned, it must be done unanimously. If the Convention wished to create a national government, it must ask for the authority to do so.

The nationalist answer was that the Convention had the right to *propose* a national government. Randolph went so far as to declare that he was "not scrupulous on the point of power" and that it would be "treason" for the Convention not to offer what the country needed. Alexander Hamilton scorned both plans as "too federal." He asserted that republican government itself was inadequate, and that the British system was the best ever devised. A government which left the states in possession of their sovereignty would fail. The central government must either "swallow up" the states or be swallowed by them. There was nothing of idealism in his conception of politics. He declared that "all the passions . . . of avarice, ambition, interest, which govern most individuals, and all public bodies" were attached to the states. Like Madison he believed all societies were divided into "the few and the many" and that each must have a check upon the other. The only source of hope he saw was that the "evils operating in the states" would soon "cure the people of their fondness for democracies." Hamilton then offered a plan which included an all-powerful executive, but only to amplify his ideas, not as a basis for discussion.

The next day, June 19, the Convention rejected the New Jersey plan by voting, seven states to three, to adhere to the plan for a national government. (*See Reading No. 2.*)

— 8 —

THE TWO COMPROMISES ON REPRESENTATION

As soon as the New Jersey plan was rejected, the Convention began debate on the first resolution of the report calling for a "national government." The nationalists tried to convince doubters that such a government would not "swallow up" the state governments. Wilson admitted that the states were necessary for "certain purposes" and Hamilton agreed that they were needed as "subordinate jurisdictions" although "as states" they ought to be abolished. King denied that the states had ever been sovereign in any real sense and insisted that much of their power should be taken from them. To Luther Martin's assertion of the sovereignty of the states, Wilson replied by reading the Declaration of Independence and then concluding that the states did not become independent of one another when it was adopted, that they "were independent, not individually, but unitedly. . . ." However, the nationalists were willing to offer a verbal concession: the word "national" would be dropped and the words "United States" substituted wherever it occurred in the report.

The Concept of the Senate. The federalist-small state group was not impressed by the arguments or the concession, and they fought so stubbornly that it took two days before the Convention could vote that Congress should consist of two houses, although this had not been in doubt from the start. On June 25 the Convention reached the crucial resolution on the senate. The federalist-small state group had won a victory on June 7 when it voted that senators should be elected by the state legislatures. The nationalists, although bitterly opposed, could now muster only the votes of Pennsylvania and Virginia against that early decision.

How long should senators serve? Nationalists Gouverneur Morris and Hamilton wanted them to serve for life while Wilson and Madison wanted as long terms as possible. Such men looked to the senate to check the more numerous house, which they took for granted would be subject to "fickleness and passion." One of the commonest assumptions of many delegates was that larger political bodies always behaved more unreasonably and unjustly than smaller ones.

But the senate was to have another function: it was to serve as the protector of property as opposed to the house, which would represent the people, or as Hamilton put it, "the poorer order of citizens. . . ." On June 26 Madison again said that in "all civilized countries the people fall into different classes having a real or supposed difference of interests," the most important being "the distinction of rich and poor." The previous day Charles Pinckney in an eloquent speech had declared that America had neither hereditary distinctions nor great extremes of wealth. Madison agreed, but he denied the implication that Americans were "one homogeneous mass." Symptoms of a "levelling spirit" had already appeared, he said, and furthermore he was worried about the future. He believed it inevitable, as did other members of the Convention, that in time the poor would outnumber "those who are placed above the feelings of indigence" and would "secretly sigh for a more equal distribution. . . ." Madison and others were convinced that eventually the United States would become like Europe, and the landed interest would be outnumbered by a propertyless population. What then, Madison asked, "will become of your government?" As a Virginian from a planter society Madison could not conceive of a stable government which was not based on land ownership. His solution was to give the landholders a permanent place in the senate, which "ought to be constituted as to protect the minority of the opulent against the majority." Hamilton agreed with Madison that "nothing like an equality of property existed" in the United States and added that "this inequality of property constituted the great and fundamental distinction in society." But as a city dweller he did not share Madison's concern for landed property, and therein lay one basis of the future split between them.

Opposition to a long senatorial term came from some nationalists, particularly those of South Carolina, and from federalists like Roger Sherman who repeated the old revolutionary argument that long terms were dangerous to the liberties of the people. The result was a compromise: senators would serve six years, with one-third going out biennially.

Representation by Population and by States.   The debate was revealing of political attitudes, but it was peripheral to the big issue of "representation." Resolutions seven and eight called for representation in both houses according to white population and three-fifths of the slaves. Federalists Yates, Lansing, Martin, and Sherman, and delegates from the small states, were determined that the states should have equal votes in at least one house, and they were supported by men from large states like Mason and Gerry who were convinced that the states must be represented as such, both as a matter of principle and as a matter of political necessity. These men began to fight in earnest on June 27 and did not give up until they won the battle on July 16. Luther Martin talked all of June 27 and part of the next day in defense of the federal system and the equality of the states. When he had done, Lansing moved to reverse the vote for proportional representation in both houses.

Doctor Johnson of Connecticut put the issue clearly. One side, he said, looked upon the states as districts of people composing a single political society. The other side held that the states existed as political societies and that a central government must be formed for them in their political capacity, as well as for the people of which they were composed. The states should have some means of defending themselves, and the solution was to have the people represented in one branch of Congress and the states in the other.

Hamilton and Madison demonstrated that Johnson's analysis of nationalist views was correct. They both denied that state sovereignty was a fact, and Hamilton even called the states "artificial beings." Madison again assured the small states that they had nothing to fear, but then inconsistently argued that they should support a national government because it would protect them from aggression by the large states. Madison charged that if the small states got their way, even in one house, it would "infuse mortality" into the constitution. The result would be incessant war, dictatorship, and foreign intervention. An occasional lucidity such as Hamilton's remark that "the truth is it is a contest for power, not for liberty" did not stop the repetition of old arguments that convinced no one. So hot did the dispute become that at one point Franklin suggested turning to prayer, but the lack of funds to pay for a minister, plus the doubtful tactic of admitting the necessity of an appeal to the Almighty, put a stop to the proposal.

Finally, on June 29, the Convention voted six to four that representation in the house should not be according to the equal rule of the Articles of Confederation. Ellsworth of Connecticut then moved that the states have equal votes in the senate. We are "partly national, partly federal," and such equality would be a reasonable compromise. But the large-state nationalists would not compromise. King of Massachusetts declared himself ready for any event, however horrible, rather than submit to a government "founded in a vicious principle of representation. . . ." The small states were equally adamant. Bedford of Delaware told the large-state delegates: "I do not, gentlemen, trust you." Madison tried to divert the Convention by again insisting that the real division was between northern and southern states. There was such a division and within a few days it, too, had to be compromised, but at the moment it was not relevant. When the vote was taken on July 2, the Convention split five states to five.

A very slight shift in certain delegations had produced the deadlock, and it seemed that it might be permanent. At last some of the nationalists realized that compromise was necessary, and General Pinckney proposed a committee to prepare one. The Convention agreed despite the opposition of the large-state nationalists. On July 5 the committee proposed: (1) that there be one representative in the house for every 40,000 inhabitants, counting the whites and three-fifths of the slaves; (2) that the states have equal votes in the senate; and (3) that money bills originate only in the house, and that the senate be denied the right to amend them. This last was offered as a concession to the large states which, it was assumed, would control the house. But Madison, Wilson, and Gouverneur Morris scoffed at it.

Morris, after picturing himself as the representative of all America, and even of the whole human race, described the civil wars, the gallows, and the sword that would result if the Convention agreed to equal votes for the states in the senate. But he soon abandoned the role of representative at large and the principle of representation according to population. Property, he said, was the main object of society, and it, too, should be counted in apportioning representatives. If it were not, the future western states would be a threat to the East. Representation should be fixed so that the Atlantic states would always control the national government. The South Carolinians, who were afraid of their own western farmers, and who had argued for representation of wealth from the start, supported Morris, as did Gerry and King of Massachusetts. Morris was made chairman of a second committee to consider the question.

On July 9 his committee proposed that the first house of representatives have 56 members, but that in the future Congress should apportion representation on the basis of both wealth and population. The committee reported that there were two objections to one representative for every 40,000 people: (1) representatives would soon be too numerous, and (2) the western states would soon "outvote the Atlantic." The latter states should keep control of the government and protect their interests by "dealing out the right of representation in safe proportions to the western states."

The Convention accepted wealth as a basis for representation without argument, but at once began a fight over the apportionment of representatives between the northern and the southern states. There had been growing opposition to counting slaves in representation among some of the northern delegates, and Paterson of New Jersey now made a head-on attack. Slaves were property; they were not represented in the states where they were owned and they should not be represented in Congress. Madison countered by declaring that all whites and blacks should be represented in the senate, which "had for one of its primary objects the guardianship of property. . . ."

Discontent with this second report on apportionment led to the election of a third committee which proposed the next day that the first house should have 65 instead of 56 members. It increased New England's representation from 14 to 17 and that of the four southern states from 21 to 23. In defending the new apportionment, King of Massachusetts said that the four New England states with 800,000 people had one-third fewer representatives than the four southern states with 700,000 people, rating blacks at five for three. He did not object to giving the South some security, but no principle would justify giving it a majority. General Pinckney replied that he did not expect the southern states to have a majority, but that they did want something like equality. If the South was to be such a minority, and the central government had the power to regulate trade, the southerners "will be nothing more than overseers for the northern states." The southerners then tried to reduce New Hampshire's representatives from three to two, and to increase their own, but the Convention rejected every motion.

The South vs. the North and the Census. By this time a good many southern delegates were convinced that northern control of Congress would mean two things: (1) a threat to their property in slaves, and (2) "navigation acts" which would exploit southern exporters for the benefit of northern shipowners. They admitted that the northern states had the majority of the population at the moment, but they believed that the southern and the new western states would have that majority in the near future. They took it for granted, too, that the northern states would never voluntarily surrender control of Congress once they had gained it. Furthermore, all of the Virginians, including Madison, and many other southern delegates, opposed any limitation on western expansion or any discrimination against new western states when they entered the union.

The southern solution was a census of population embedded in the Constitution. Edmund Randolph proposed that the first Congress be required to take a census within one year, and at regular intervals thereafter, to determine changes in wealth and population of the states, and then to apportion representation accordingly. He at once accepted a proposal that all the whites and three-fifths of the slaves be counted in such a census. Randolph argued that the apportionment of representatives without a census would be mere guesswork and that it would place power in the hands of a part of America that would not always be entitled to it. Since such power would never be surrendered voluntarily, Congress should have no discretion. The Convention must guarantee alterations in representation by constitutional means. Some alarmed southerners went further. Butler of South Carolina insisted that slaves should be counted equally with freemen "in a government which was instituted principally for the protection of property, and was itself to be supported by property."

Gouverneur Morris led those northerners opposed to a required census, but his brilliance in debate, utterly unchecked by consistency, was not convincing. He argued that the representatives of the people should not be fettered, yet he had no faith in either. As a northerner and a large-state representative he wanted representation according to population, but he opposed application of the principle to the western states. At the same time he argued that wealth should be counted as well. Madison told him that while he was telling the South it should have confidence in the northern majority, he was trying to create a jealousy of a future western majority. "To reconcile the gentleman with himself, it must be imagined that he determined the human character by the points of the compass."

The Convention agreed that there should be a census of white population and then debated whether three-fifths of the slaves should be included. Wilson, who had originally proposed that three-fifths be counted, now argued that he could not see how the admission of three-fifths could be explained, although he agreed on the need of compromise. King of Massachusetts was opposed to basing representation on population in any case. Morris declared himself reduced to the dilemma of doing injustice to the southern states or to human nature, and must, therefore, do it to the states. He piously insisted that he could never agree to the encouragement of the slave trade by counting the slaves in representation. The Convention rejected a census of slaves and then rejected the idea of a census entirely.

The next day the agile Morris added to his original proposal that representation be based on wealth and population the proviso that taxation be in proportion to representation. The presumption was that this would discourage the states from demanding more representatives which would in turn mean more taxes. He at once agreed to limit the rule to direct taxation, saying it should not be applied to taxes on imports, exports, and consumption.

The southerners agreed that the principle of relating direct taxation to representation was a good one, but they were more suspicious of Morris and the northerners than ever. Butler again insisted that all slaves be counted in representation. General Pinckney, alarmed at Morris's attack on slavery and his talk of taxing exports, declared his support for a required census. Davie of North Carolina brought the debate to a halt by saying it was high time to speak out. Some members meant to deprive the southern states of representatives for their slaves, even three-fifths of them, and North Carolina would never agree. If the "eastern states" meant to exclude slaves, "the business was at an end."

The threat of a walkout brought sudden talk of compromise. The Connecticut delegates had shown willingness to compromise with the South from the beginning, and Doctor Johnson now urged that all population, both white and black, be counted in representation, and Ellsworth moved that three-fifths of the slaves as well as white population be counted in apportioning both representatives and direct taxes. Morris urged the New England and the southern states to compromise but then declared that the people of Pennsylvania would never agree to the representation of slaves.

Once more Randolph insisted that Congress should have no discretion, and again he moved that a regular census be made a part of the Constitution and that representation be based on white population and three-fifths of all others. There had to be security for representation of slaves since some delegates wanted to exclude them altogether. James Wilson countered with a formula which he said would make the representation of slaves less offensive by making it indirect. He proposed that representation should be in proportion to direct taxation, which, in turn, should be based on the white population and three-fifths of all others, as determined by a regular census. The Convention accepted the formula and voted that the census must be taken every ten years. In slightly altered form, the formula appears in Article I of the Constitution.

This agreement meant that the former vote including wealth as a basis must be reversed. Most members believed that population was a rough index of wealth, as they had ever since 1776, but Morris disagreed to the end. He predicted that the southern states and the new western states would join in an agrarian persecution of commerce. He would, therefore, vote for the "vicious principle" of equality in the senate to give some protection to the commercial states of the North. Butler replied that "the security the southern states want is that their Negroes may not be taken from them," but he admitted complacently that "the people and strength of America are evidently bearing southwardly and southwestwardly."

The southerners who had originally supported wealth as a basis of representation were now willing to abandon it. They had won representation based on three-fifths of their slaves and the guarantee that the population growth they expected would soon be reflected in the house of representatives. Nationalist leaders like Madison and Wilson had opposed wealth from the start. They were convinced that representation according to population in both houses was the only way to eliminate state control over the central government, and they were not unaware of the weight it would give to their own states. Wilson denied that property was the sole object of society, but he warned that representation according to population in the house was no justification for letting a "vicious principle into the second branch." The Convention agreed unanimously to drop "wealth." Thus was concluded the first of two basic compromises—that between the free and the slave states.

Equality of the States in the Senate. However, the Convention was back where it started on July 2 with the deadlock vote on the equality of the states in the senate. Luther Martin demanded an end to talk and a vote on the whole compromise proposal of July 5, and he was supported by many others even though they did not agree with all its details. Madison, Wilson, and King repeated all their old arguments against state equality and pled for even further debate. The only delay they won was over Sunday. On Monday, July 16, Connecticut, New Jersey, Delaware, Maryland, and North Carolina voted for equality. Pennsylvania, Virginia, South Carolina, and Georgia opposed. The Massachusetts delegation was divided, with King and Gorham opposing compromise to the end while Gerry and Strong supported it. In addition, the compromise included the apportionment of representatives among the states according to the number of white inhabitants, plus three-fifths of all others (as determined by a required census every decade), and the exclusive control over money bills by the house of representatives.

The Convention then adjourned until the next day to give the large states time to consider what to do in the "present solemn crisis" and the small states time to propose "means of conciliation." The next day the delegates of the large states held an informal meeting. They could not agree. Some proposed to offer a constitution of their own to the country; others insisted they must accept the victory of the small states. Since they could not unite on a program, they tacitly agreed to go ahead writing a constitution which included equal votes for the states in a senate elected by the state legislatures.

The delegates from the small states, and those from the large states who believed that the central government must be partly federal in structure, were on the side of political realism: the states were facts that could not be ignored. The victory of July 16 recognized this political reality and kept the Convention in being. There were to be many other disputes, some crucial, in the weeks ahead, but one of the greatest obstacles to success was removed.

— 9 —

THE POWER OF CONGRESS

Within ten days after the compromise of July 16 the Convention completed debate on the balance of the resolutions of June 19 and elected a committee to draft a formal constitution. During those ten days the debates centered around two basic demands of the nationalist leaders. They continued to insist that there should be no limitation on the power of Congress over the states, and at the same time they sought to place sharp limitations upon the power of Congress within the central government itself by establishing a powerful executive.

Power over the States. A key issue was the constitutional statement of the powers of Congress. Should they be specifically enumerated as in the Articles of Confederation or based upon a general grant? There was common agreement that Congress should have all the powers of Congress under the Articles. But should it also have power to legislate in all cases where the states were "incompetent" or the "harmony" of the union might be interrupted? This had been proposed in the Virginia resolutions on May 29, but there was strong opposition

to such vagueness, and on July 16 the Convention split
five states to five.

The next day Sherman tried to draw a line between
national and state power. He proposed that Congress
have the power to make laws binding the people in matters concerning the common interests of the union, but
not the power to intervene in matters of "internal police"
which concerned only the states and did not concern
the "general welfare" of the United States. James Wilson
supported the motion, perhaps because he saw a significance in "general welfare" which others, including Sherman, did not. But Gouverneur Morris's argument was
more convincing: the "internal police" of the states
ought to be interfered with in such cases as paper money.
Bedford of Delaware, a strong nationalist after the vote
for equality in the senate, then moved that Congress have
the power to legislate "in all cases for the general interests of the union. . . ." Randolph warned that such a
wording meant the power to violate both state laws and
state constitutions, but the Convention agreed to the motion.

The nationalists thus won a victory, but they soon lost
on a principle which they believed to be the very essence
of control over the states: Congress's veto of state legislation which in its opinion violated the Constitution. The
Convention had accepted the principle on May 31, but a
few days later rejected an attempt of Pinckney, Wilson,
and Madison to add the power to veto *all* state laws.
Then, on July 17, the Convention abolished Congress's
veto power. This time, Gouverneur Morris, who had
been absent throughout June, disagreed with the other nationalists, while such men as Sherman opposed the veto
as a matter of course. Madison was its most persistent
defender. It was too late, he argued, for Congress or the
courts to set aside a state law after it had been passed
and the damage done. The Convention ignored his appeals and rejected all his later efforts to restore the veto.
He remained convinced that the lack of the veto was a
fatal defect which would make it impossible to enforce
the restrictions upon state economic legislation embodied in the Constitution.

The alternative to the congressional veto of state laws
was enforcement of restraints by the courts. Luther

Martin offered a provision taken almost verbatim from the New Jersey plan: the acts of Congress and United States treaties would be "the supreme law of the respective states" and be binding upon the state courts, any state laws to the contrary. The Convention accepted Martin's motion. Although the nationalists were opposed to any jurisdiction for the state courts in national affairs, they did not protest at the time. Later on, however, they were able to clothe the "supreme law" idea with a significance quite different than Martin intended.

The Convention was agreed that there should be a supreme court, and most delegates assumed from the start that it would have the power to rule on the constitutionality of state and national laws. But the Convention differed sharply about the role of inferior national courts. Early in June the federalists and the South Carolina nationalists had persuaded the Convention to vote that the power of Congress to establish inferior courts should be discretionary rather than mandatory as in the Virginia resolutions. In July they again argued that the state courts could perform all the necessary functions, leaving appeal open to the supreme court. Again the nationalists asserted that inferior national courts throughout the union were absolutely necessary to the success of the system and that the state courts should have no jurisdiction. However, the decision made in June was left unchanged and found its way into the Constitution. Thus it was left to party politics rather than to a constitutional provision to determine the role of inferior national courts in the first decades under the new Constitution.

The resolution guaranteeing a republican constitution and the existing laws of the states, which had appeared first in the report of June 19, caused some confusion. But when Gouverneur Morris objected to guaranteeing the laws of such a state as Rhode Island, Randolph and Wilson explained what was intended. The purpose, said Randolph, was the suppression of domestic rebellion. Wilson, characteristically, offered a rewording to soften the tone but not the intent: each state would be guaranteed a republican form of government and protected against foreign and domestic violence. The Convention, with Shays's Rebellion ever in mind, agreed without dissent.

Method of Ratification. But there was a basic disagreement over the resolution calling for ratification by state conventions. This method had been suggested before the Convention met and was a part of the Virginia resolutions. In early June all the federalists had supported ratification by the state legislatures and all the nationalists ratification by conventions. They took the same positions in July and repeated arguments which combined high theory with a concern for practical politics. Again the nationalists urged the ultimate authority of the people, and they were supported by George Mason, who echoed the words he had written in the Virginia Bill of Rights in 1776. The extreme nationalists carried their arguments to such lengths as to justify Gerry's comment that they were trying to prove that even the Articles of Confederation and the state constitutions were unconstitutional.

The federalists again insisted that ratification by legislatures was the only legal and constitutional means of procedure. Ellsworth of Connecticut supported a strong central government, but he refused to accept the extremists' arguments. However it got that way, he said, the United States was in fact a federal society with a constitution which provided a method of amendment. He moved for ratification by the state legislatures. Gouverneur Morris, whose verbal agility sometimes led him to take mutually exclusive positions within moments, could also be direct and to the point. Ellsworth's motion was wrong because it assumed that "we are proceeding on the basis of the Confederation. This Convention is unknown to the Confederation."

Some of the nationalists talked practical politics, not theory. They declared that ratification could not be gained within the existing framework and that the requirement of unanimous ratification by state legislatures must be avoided. Such men convinced the Convention in July, and again later, that ratification by less than all the states was the only hope of securing the adoption of any constitution offered by the Convention.

Limits on Congressional Power. The purpose of the extreme nationalists, as Madison said at one point, was to create a Congress with more power over the states than the British Parliament had ever had over the colonies. But at the same time the nationalists made it clear that they distrusted an all-powerful Congress within the central government as much as they did the all-powerful state legislatures. The Virginia resolutions, and the resolutions of the national plan which followed, provided for a central government dominated by Congress, and this the nationalists now sought to reverse. In the course of the attempt they abandoned theoretical talk of "balanced government" or twisted theory to justify their purpose.

Conversely, the federalists, the middle-of-the-roaders like Mason and Dickinson, and nationalists such as Rutledge who argued for limitations on Congress's power over the states, now insisted that Congress must be supreme within the central government. They clung to the original propositions of the Virginia resolutions, and they too argued for "balanced government." What they displayed in fact was that distrust of executive power which was a basic part of the revolutionary tradition and which was embodied in the state constitutions, the Articles of Confederation, and in the national plan as it existed in mid-July.

The nationalists wanted a powerful executive to act as a check upon the legislative branch of government. Their conception of the presidency was evident early in the Convention, but they amplified it in specific terms during the last two weeks of July. Most of them agreed (1) that the president should have an absolute veto on the acts of Congress; (2) that the judges of the national courts should share in the veto power; (3) that the president rather than Congress should appoint judges; (4) that the president should not be elected by Congress; (5) that he should be eligible for more than one term.

In June, Madison and Wilson had tried to transfer the appointment of judges from Congress to the president, but only managed to give it to the senate. They tried again in July, but again they failed. In June the Convention had denied judges a share in the veto power, agreeing with Gerry that since judges would decide upon the constitutionality of laws, they should not share in the lawmaking power. In July, Madison, Wilson, and Morris tried to restore the judges to a share in the veto, talking at length of the danger of unchecked legislatures. Madison argued that even if the judges acted with the president, the two branches together would be too weak to defend themselves against legislative encroachment, for what was true of state legislatures would be even more true of Congress. Morris insisted that public liberty was in "greater danger from legislative usurpations than from any other source." It was useless, he said, to suppose that Congress would not pass bad laws providing for paper money, the remission of debts, and the like. Wilson supported Madison's argument that the principle of separation of powers was not involved and that the president and the judges must act together to "balance the single weight of the legislature." The Convention refused to change its decision and again voted that the president alone should exercise the veto. Furthermore, it voted that a two-thirds vote of each house could override a veto. Wilson's proposal of an absolute veto smelled too much of "monarchy" to a majority of the members.

The national plan in mid-July provided that Congress should elect the president for one term of seven years. During the next two weeks a variety of contradictory votes were taken on a variety of proposals which included election by state legislatures, by electors chosen by the people, and even choice by lot. The spokesmen of the Madison-Wilson-Morris group opposed election by Congress with all their eloquence. They repeated their arguments about the danger of unchecked legislative power which would come into being if Congress elected the president. Madison pointed to the "omnipotent" state legislatures and the governors who were "ciphers" as the worst of all examples. At one point he summed up the extreme nationalist position succinctly:

> The legislatures of the states had betrayed a strong propensity to a variety of pernicious measures. One object of the national legislature was to control this propensity. One object of the national executive, so far as it would have a negative on the laws, was to control the national legislature, so far as it might be infected with a similar propensity.

And Madison and his group made it plain they believed Congress would have a "similar propensity." The only solution they could see was popular election. Wilson had argued for it from the start, and in time Madison and Morris came to agree. No one pointed out the paradox of having "the people's choice" check representatives who were not to be trusted because they in turn were the choice of "the people." By July 26, however, the Convention was back where it had started on May 29: it once more voted that Congress should elect the president.

— 10 —

THE FIRST DRAFT OF THE CONSTITUTION

On July 26 the Convention adjourned until August 6. Three days before it had agreed to turn all the proceedings over to a committee of detail to prepare a draft constitution. It elected Rutledge of South Carolina, Randolph of Virginia, Wilson of Pennsylvania, Ellsworth of Connecticut, and Gorham of Massachusetts. Wilson was the only representative of the extreme nationalist group. The committee was weighted on the side of the middle-of-the-road nationalists, and it was weighted too on the side of the South. The constitution it presented to the Convention on August 6 reflected these facts, which meant new debates on old points and created the need for more basic compromises. Nevertheless, the draft constitution was a major step forward.

It consisted of a preamble and 23 articles divided into 41 sections. In writing the draft the committee of detail used a wide variety of sources including the plans submitted to the Convention, the resolutions adopted by it, the state constitutions, and large portions of the Articles of Confederation. On the whole the committee steered a middle course between the extremists on both sides.

The draft enumerated the powers of Congress instead of basing its power on a general grant as the extreme nationalists had demanded. The 18 powers given included many taken bodily from the Articles and others which the Convention had not discussed. Furthermore, the draft placed specific restraints upon the power of Congress, something unheard of (aside from the presidential veto) in the previous debates. It gave the senate several powers in addition to its legislative authority and spelled out the duties and responsibilities of the president. The jurisdiction of the national court, like the powers of Congress, was given in specific detail rather than based on the general statement voted earlier in the Convention.

The relation between the central government and the state governments was defined far more sharply than in the prior resolutions adopted by the Convention. As an alternative to the congressional veto, the draft provided specific restraints upon state economic legislation and additional ones taken from the Articles. At the same time the states were given some guarantee of their sovereignty. The central government could not intervene in a state unless requested to do so by its legislature; the state legislatures were given the power to initiate amendments to the Constitution by requesting Congress to call a convention; and new states were to be admitted to the union upon a basis of equality with the old ones.

The draft constitution shifted the work of the Convention from what had been largely a discussion of general principles to a debate over the specific details of governmental organization. The Convention went through the draft, article by article, as it had the previous resolutions, accepting large portions, rejecting others, and constantly making verbal changes. As the Convention progressed the delegates continued to appeal to history, although they often drew quite different conclusions from it. They made, too, a variety of prophecies. Whatever the merits of their predictions about the future course of American society, they were at best average prophets when it came to estimating how specific constitutional devices would work. Some of the details disputed most hotly turned out to be of little consequence to posterity while others that were almost ignored at the time proved to be of the utmost importance.

The Preamble. The draft began with a preamble stating that "We the people of the states of," listing each state individually from New Hampshire to Georgia, "do ordain, declare, and establish the following Constitution for the government of ourselves and our posterity." The Convention agreed to it without comment, although later the preamble was revised and elaborated. Among other things, "We the People of the United States" was substituted for the names of the separate states. During ratification opponents of the Constitution asserted the wording was proof that the Constitution provided for a national government and that the intention of its authors was to destroy the states. And later on the preamble was used to support the argument that the Constitution was the creation of the people of the nation as a whole, not the creation of the people of the separate states. Such an interpretation was consistent with the argument of the large-state nationalists early in the Convention, but if anyone in the Convention recognized the significance of the preamble for later constitutional interpretation, he did not say so. The reason for the change in language was simple. The Convention had agreed that ratification by nine states would be enough to put the Constitution into operation. No one could guess which states would or would not ratify and to list them all by name would be to run political risks that the members were too wise to take.

The Qualifications of the Electors and of the Elected. The first serious debates came with the discussion of the qualifications of voters for members of the house. The draft provided that voters in each state should have the same qualifications as the voters for the most numerous branch of its legislature. Since qualifications varied from state to state this was a sensible solution. But Gouverneur Morris at once proposed that the suffrage be limited to landowners. In the ensuing debate Morris, Dickinson, and Madison all reiterated the common belief that in the future the great majority of the American people would be propertyless and that some property qualification for voting would be needed to protect the minority of property owners. If adopted, Madison wanted such a qualification placed in the Constitution, not left to the discretion of Congress, but he was doubtful of how the states would receive it. Furthermore, the theoretical argument for a landowning qualification was badly shaken because the attacks on "property," which had done so much to produce the Convention, were coming from small farmers who owned land and hence could vote. As one delegate pointed out, the "mechanics" behaved at least as well at the polls as the landowners.

There were also practical obstacles. Many states had extended the suffrage beyond the freehold qualification, and a few had abandoned the property qualification entirely. To impose a national requirement would exclude men of wealth who were not landowners and many "mechanics" who were accustomed to voting. As Gorham put it, the Convention must consult the "rooted prejudice" of the people if it expected them to approve its work. The Convention rejected Morris's motion, thus leaving the extent of suffrage entirely in the hands of the states.

The draft provided also that the states should fix the time, manner, and place of electing representatives and senators, but that Congress might at any time alter their decisions. Pinckney and Rutledge proposed that Congress have no power at all over elections, but the Convention rejected the idea overwhelmingly. In final form, the Constitution permitted Congress to alter state regulations, except for the place of electing senators. The provision was bitterly attacked in the ratifying conventions, many agreeing with Luther Martin's assertion that its purpose was "the utter extinction and abolition of all state governments."

Qualifications for members of Congress was a thornier issue. Age had been the only one discussed and agreed to prior to the draft constitution: 30 years for senators and 25 for representatives. The draft provided in addition that representatives must have been citizens for three years and senators for four, and be residents of the states from whence chosen. The citizenship requirement provoked a violent outburst against "foreigners" and for once allied such men as George Mason and Gouverneur Morris. Mason moved that representatives be citizens for seven years because he "did not choose to let foreigners and adventurers make laws for us and govern us." The Convention agreed. Gouverneur Morris then declared that senators should be citizens for fourteen years because he did not wish to see "those philosophical gentlemen, those citizens of the world as they call themselves . . . in our public councils." Such statements were a blow in the teeth of such foreign-born members of the Convention as James Wilson, Alexander Hamilton, and Robert Morris. Wilson argued against such illiberality, and he was supported by Franklin and Madison. The Convention temporarily agreed on nine years' citizenship for senators and three years' for representatives.

Property qualifications for legislators had been discussed from time to time, and the committee of detail had been instructed to establish a constitutional provision. But the committee could not agree, and so it gave Congress the power. Charles Pinckney asserted that Congress should not have this power, but that qualifications were needed. He suggested at least a hundred thousand dollars for the president, half that for judges, and proportionate amounts for legislators. His motion was rejected by "so general a *no*, that the states were not called." It was obvious to most members that a uniform rule would not apply equally to all the states, and that to embed a property qualification in the Constitution might cause trouble in the future. Furthermore, a constitutional provision would arouse political opposition in the states. Nor were the members willing to trust any future Congress. The only way out of the dilemma was to abandon the property qualification entirely, and the Convention did so.

The question of religious qualifications for officeholders arose only incidentally. Most of the revolutionary constitutions of the states had them. In six states one had to be a Protestant. In Massachusetts it was enough to be a Christian, but in Delaware one had to believe in the Trinity and the divine inspiration of the Scriptures. The Articles of Confederation had ignored religious qualifications as had all the various resolutions and plans submitted to the Convention, including the draft constitution of August 6. Given the religious diversity of the states, the mere suggestion of the idea would have been political dynamite. Furthermore, the members of the Convention were far more liberal in their religious views than many ordinary Americans.

Political realism and religious liberalism combined to make two important changes in the draft constitution. It had provided that national as well as state officials and legislators must take an oath to support the Constitution.

On August 30 the Convention agreed without dissent to add "or affirmation" after "oath," and it added Charles Pinckney's proposal that "no religious test shall ever be required as a qualification to any office or public trust under the authority of the United States." After the Convention some opponents of the Constitution professed to see this as opening the way for atheism and even worse evils, but they clearly did not represent the majority of the American voters, who demanded a bill of rights which included, among other things, a guarantee that Congress should never interfere with religion.

The Organization of Congress. The details of the internal organization of Congress were settled rapidly, although with much quibbling. Congressmen were accorded the privileges long since claimed by Parliament and by the colonial legislatures, and embodied in the state constitutions and the Articles of Confederation: freedom of speech in debate; freedom from arrest during sessions except for treason, felony, or breach of the peace; the right to be judge of the elections and qualifications of members; the right to punish them for disorderly behavior, and to expel a member by a two-thirds vote. It was agreed that each house should keep and publish a journal and that the votes should be entered when demanded by one-fifth of the members present. Neither house could adjourn for more than three days without the consent of the other, nor could Congress move to another place during a session. The president, like the state governors, had no control except that, like some of them, he could convene special sessions.

The only serious debate concerned compensation. From the beginning the Convention had voted that congressmen should be paid from the national treasury to free them from dependence on the states. But the draft constitution provided that they should be paid by their states as under the Articles. All the old arguments between the nationalists and the supporters of the states were repeated, and then the Convention rejected state payment once more. But should congressmen fix their own salaries? Early in the Convention, Madison had said this would be "indecent" and that salaries should be fixed in relation to the price of wheat or some other commodity. After considering five dollars a day and also minimum salaries fixed in the Constitution, the Convention finally left it up to Congress—and to posterity—to judge if its use of the power was "indecent."

In keeping with the opposition to multiple officeholding so prevalent in the revolutionary era (embodied in the Articles of Confederation and most of the state constitutions), the draft forbade members of Congress to hold any other government offices, and denied senators any office for one year after the end of their terms. Charles Pinckney declared that such a restriction was "degrading," particularly to the senate which should be "a school of public ministers, a nursery of statesmen. . . ." He proposed that legislators be excluded only from those offices for which they received pay. Mason "ironically proposed" to strike out the whole section to encourage "that exotic corruption which might not otherwise thrive so well in the American soil—for completing that aristocracy which was probably in the contemplation of some among us. . . ." Few friends, he said, would be lost to the system by "giving premiums to a mercenary and depraved ambition." A few delegates argued that the only way to attract men to Congress would be to offer them additional government offices, but the majority was not convinced. Pinckney's motion was rejected, and the Constitution provided that congressmen could not be appointed to offices created, or offices given pay increases, during their terms, nor could officeholders be members of Congress. The restriction, of course, did not apply to ex-congressmen or ex-officeholders.

The two major disputes revolved around the veto power of the president and the control of money bills. From the beginning the extreme nationalists demanded an absolute veto for the president, and some of them insisted that supreme court judges share in the power. On August 15, Madison, for the third time, moved that judges participate, but the opposition, which disapproved of "judges meddling in politics and parties," had its way. Then Morris once more argued that a president elected by Congress must have an absolute veto to check legislative usurpation. All the old arguments were repeated, but most of the delegates were bored with them. The Convention finally agreed, as a concession, to require a three-fourths instead of a two-thirds vote to override a veto. But on

September 12, after agreeing to the election of the president by electors instead of by Congress, the Convention restored the two-thirds vote despite the bitter-end opposition of Morris and Madison.

The members of the Convention regarded the control of money bills as fundamental in any government. The compromise of July 16 had combined equality of the states in the senate with the grant of exclusive control over money bills to the house and had denied the senate the power to alter or amend them. It had been offered as a concession to the large states which would control the house, but the nationalists from those states scorned it. The draft constitution contained the compromise, but on August 8 the section concerning money bills was voted out, thus giving the senate equal power with the house in money matters, including the right to originate money bills. The controversy thus started was not settled until near the end of the Convention.

The belief in the control of money bills by the elected representatives of the people was deeply rooted in Anglo-American tradition and political practice. In the 17th century the House of Commons had asserted its exclusive right to levy taxes and to control the expenditure of the money raised. Every colonial assembly had copied the arguments and the methods of the Commons in struggles with councils and governors, and by 1763, in practice if not in law, most of them had won control over money bills. The argument that Americans could be taxed only by representatives of their own choosing was a very foundation of the war for independence. Most of the first state constitutions gave the lower houses the exclusive power of originating money bills, and some of them denied the senates the power to alter or amend them.

The proposed senate in 1787 clearly represented the state legislatures, not the people, but the Convention had now voted to give it equal power in money matters.

The older revolutionary leaders such as Gerry, Sherman, Dickinson, and Mason clung tenaciously to the revolutionary ideal that taxation and representation must go together. In the end, even Washington switched his vote and joined his old friend Mason in opposition to equal power for the senate. These men argued that the senate did not represent the people, that it would be an all-powerful aristocracy. (At this stage the senate had the power to make treaties, appoint judges and ambassadors, and to set up courts to settle disputes over lands, in addition to its legislative powers.) They warned that to tamper with tradition would endanger ratification. However, they were willing to compromise and allow the senate to amend money bills.

Most of the extreme nationalist leaders were unmoved by such revolutionary theories as those concerning the relation of representation to taxation, and they had made it clear that they did not trust the elected representatives of the people, either in the state legislatures or in the future Congress. From the beginning they had conceived of the senate as an institution which would protect the large propertied minority from the small-propertied, and in time, propertyless, majority of the people of the nation. Control of money bills was of the very essence of such a function, and some of the extremists went so far as to demand that the senate itself should have exclusive power. Again and again they rejected compromises, but in the end they were forced to yield to an old and potent tradition and practice. The Constitution gave the house the exclusive right to originate money bills, but provided that the senate could amend them. The members of the Convention seemed not to realize that the right to amend meant virtually equal power for the senate, but the opponents of the Constitution in the ratifying conventions were clear on this point—and right.

The Powers of Congress.   The constitutional statement of the powers of Congress had been a basic issue from the outset, but the nationalists now accepted without argument the enumeration they had formerly opposed. The Convention rapidly agreed to most of the powers given, but made occasional verbal and sometimes decisive changes, and eventually added other powers to the list.

The basic power was the power to tax, which Congress under the Articles had lacked. Although it had not been discussed previously in the Convention, the delegates took it for granted that the tax power would be given to the new Congress. The first of the enumerated powers was "to lay and collect taxes, duties, imposts, and excises." This was agreed to after a brief and violent debate over denial of the power to tax exports which occurred later in the draft. The power to levy direct taxes and poll taxes was limited by the requirements that both must be apportioned according to a census of all white and three-fifths of "all other persons" except non-taxpaying Indians. The Convention apparently was not clear about direct taxes, for when King asked "what was the precise meaning of *direct* taxation?" Madison noted succinctly: "no one answered." The Convention did know that poll taxes were vastly unpopular, and they were bitterly opposed in the ratifying conventions. However, the Convention agreed to both taxes, apparently on the assumption that the taxing power should not be limited even if portions of it were not used. Congress in fact levied very few direct taxes before the twentieth century and has never attempted a poll tax.

Within a few days the Convention agreed without debate or dissent to clauses giving Congress the power to establish uniform rules of naturalization, regulate commerce with foreign nations and among the states, coin money, fix standards of weights and measures, establish postoffices (it added post roads), regulate the value of foreign coins, make rules for captures on land and water, define and punish piracies and felonies on the high seas, and punish counterfeiting and offenses against the laws of nations.

But the clause empowering Congress to "borrow money and emit bills on the credit of the United States" aroused the antagonism to paper money which had done so much to produce the meeting of the Convention. Gouverneur Morris was widely supported when he moved to eliminate the power to issue paper money. He said that "the monied interest" would oppose the Constitution unless this were done, to which Mercer of Maryland replied that the "people of property" would support it anyway and that it was "impolitic" to purchase their further support "with the loss of the opposite class of citizens." The only serious objection was that an absolute prohibition might be harmful in a future emergency. George Mason pointed out that the war for independence could not have been fought if paper money had been prohibited. The objection was brushed aside, the great majority agreeing with John Langdon who said he would rather reject the whole plan than retain the three words "and emit bills." Or as Read put it more colorfully: if the power were not denied it "would be as alarming as the mark of the Beast in Revelations." The words were eliminated, only Maryland and New Jersey voting to retain them.

From the beginning the extreme nationalists had demanded unlimited power to intervene in a state, and to authorize such intervention the Convention had agreed to guarantee a republican form of government and to protect the states against domestic and foreign violence. The draft constitution specifically gave Congress the power to "subdue a rebellion" in any state, but *only* upon the request of its legislature. An additional article guaranteed a republican form of government and provided for protection against "domestic violence," but again such protection could be given only upon the request of a state legislature. These two limitations produced the usual debate between the supporters of national and of state power.

The nationalists now insisted that the power of the central government must be unlimited, while men like Gerry fulminated against "letting loose the myrmidons of the United States on a state without its own consent." The power to subdue rebellion was dropped entirely when the states split evenly. But when the article guaranteeing a republican form of government and protection against invasion and domestic violence was taken up at the end of August, the nationalists again failed to eliminate the need for a call from a state legislature. However, they were able to add that the call might come also from a state governor, and the Convention rejected Luther Martin's motion that the governor could act only during a recess of a legislature. But at the very end, section 4 of Article IV of the Constitution was amended to read that protection from "domestic violence" was to be given by the "United States" upon call from a state legislature, or from a governor when the legislature could not be convened. This provision might be interpreted as a victory for the supporters of state legislative authority, but left it vague as to what agency of the "United States" could respond. The right had been denied to Congress and it had not been given to the president. In time, presidents were to exercise the power and, in addition, to ignore the provision that intervention must await a request from a state.

The military powers were stated succinctly: Congress was to "make war," "raise armies," "build and equip fleets," and "call forth the aid of the militia, in order to execute the laws of the Union, enforce treaties, suppress insurrections, and repel invasions." Pinckney at once proposed that the senate alone have the power to make war, while his colleague Butler declared that the president should have it, to which a shocked Gerry replied that he "never expected to hear in a republic" such a motion. Madison and Gerry moved that the words should be "declare war," not "make war," and after much quibbling the Convention agreed. Butler and Gerry then joined forces to urge that Congress should have the power to make peace as well, but the Convention rejected the motion unanimously. The other military powers were agreed to with verbal changes and the Convention added one taken from the Articles of Confederation: to make rules for the government and regulation of land and naval forces.

It was inevitable that the discussion of military power would awaken the ancient distrust of professional soldiers which had been so powerful a force during the war for independence and which had helped prevent the establishment of a standing army at the end of the war. Gerry reflected the feeling of New England when he proposed that the peacetime army be limited to a few thousand, and he was supported by Luther Martin. The suggestion was ridiculed and rejected unanimously although a partial concession, based on tradition, was agreed to. One weapon Parliament had used to achieve victory over the Crown was to make appropriations only from year to year, and the colonial legislatures had copied the practice in developing their own power. In particular, the House of Commons had applied the principle to military appropriations in the "mutiny acts." George Mason was an eloquent opponent of "perpetual revenue," which, he said, "must of necessity subvert the liberty of any country." No one objected to the principle, but in the end the Convention applied it only to military matters. To the power to raise and support armies it added that "no appropriation of money to that use shall be for a longer term than two years."

The power to call forth the state militia created a far more heated and protracted debate. To many Americans

the state militia composed of "citizen soldiers" were sym-
bols of the freedom and independence of the states. They
believed that such militia made a standing army unnecessary and above all that the central government should
have no control over them. The great majority of the
Convention, however, had nothing but contempt for militia, and no one was more contemptuous than the presiding
officer, George Washington. The Convention supported
Mason's motion that Congress provide laws for the discipline and regulation of the militia although it left the
appointment of officers to the states. Ellsworth, Sherman,
and Dickinson all objected that the states would never
give up control, and if the Constitution provided for it,
Gerry cried, "the plan will have as black a mark as was
set on Cain." The Convention ignored them and voted
that Congress could call forth the militia and provide for
arming and disciplining those in the service of the United
States.

The last of the enumerated powers was a contribution
of the committee of detail. It gave Congress power "to
make all laws that shall be necessary and proper for carrying into execution the foregoing powers, and all other
powers vested, by this Constitution, in the government of
the United States, or in any department or officer thereof."
On August 20 the Convention accepted the clause without
debate or dissent. When the Constitution was published,
its opponents at once labeled this the "sweeping clause"
and asserted that its purpose was to give Congress unlimited power. The supporters of the Constitution insisted
that its purpose was merely to authorize Congress to carry
its enumerated powers into effect, and that it had no other
significance. But men on all sides at the time were thoroughly aware of the idea of "implied powers," and it did
not take long for Congress to begin legislating in areas
apart from the enumerated powers granted to it.

Meanwhile, Madison, Pinckney, Morris, and others suggested many additional powers. On August 18, Madison
and Pinckney proposed, among other things, that Congress have power to dispose of United States land, rule
the seat of government, grant charters of incorporation,
issue copyrights to authors and patents to inventors, and
establish a university. These and other suggestions were
turned over to the committee of detail, but of all the

powers suggested, the Convention adopted only three in addition to those in the draft constitution. Congress was given the authority to issue copyrights and patents for "limited times," to rule a seat of government which would not be more than ten miles square, and to dispose of and make rules for the territory and other property of the United States.

Meanwhile, nothing had been said of the national debt, which had been a constitutional issue as well as an economic problem ever since the middle of the war for independence. Men of all shades of opinion were convinced that the government which paid the debt would be the ultimate political power in the nation. Between 1781 and 1783, Robert Morris, as superintendent of finance, had led a group of men determined to create a powerful central government, a group which believed it must have the active support of the public creditors and of monied men in general to achieve success. Morris therefore had led a campaign to give Congress the power to tax so that it could pay the debt, and he proposed to assume the state war debts as well.

The opponents of a strong central government also believed that the "power of the purse" would determine the locus of political power, and they defeated Morris's program. Furthermore, many of the states, partly from political conviction and partly because of pressure from creditors, began assuming more and more of the national debt owing to their citizens. This process was well under way in 1787. Robert Morris and the men who had supported him from 1781 to 1783—Hamilton, Wilson, Madison, and Gouverneur Morris—all sat in the Convention, but none of them raised the issue of the national debt. It was raised by the South Carolina and Massachusetts delegates, whose chief concern was with their state debts. Some states had done much to pay their debts, but those two had not. It is worth noting that in 1790 congressmen from those two states threatened to break up the union if Congress did not assume the state debts at once.

On August 18, Charles Pinckney said that some provision should be made for the payment of the debt and that a pledge should be given to the creditors that the public faith would not be violated in the new Constitution. Rutledge of South Carolina then moved the appointment of a "grand committee" to consider the assumption of state debts, and he was seconded by Pinckney and by King of Massachusetts. Rutledge said that the accounts between the states and the union would never be settled, that justice demanded assumption because the debts had been contracted in the common defense, that assumption was necessary because the states were giving up taxes on imports, and that "it was politic," for assumption would conciliate the people. King added pointedly that the state creditors were an "active and formidable party" who would otherwise oppose the Constitution.

The "grand committee" was appointed, and three days later it proposed that Congress have power to fulfill the engagements of the Confederation Congress and to pay the debts of the United States and of the states incurred during the late war "for the common defense and general welfare." Gerry at once insisted that Congress be required to pay the debts, not merely given the power to do so. He extolled the merits of the public creditors, but warned that the states which had paid a large part of their debts would object to being saddled with the debts of those states which had not. Gouverneur Morris then moved that Congress "shall discharge the debts," and the Convention agreed unanimously.

This vote brought out the distaste for speculators in the public debt which some few members felt and which was widespread among the people. Butler of South Carolina demanded reconsideration. He charged that requiring Congress to pay the debt would mean payment to "blood-suckers who had speculated on the distresses of others" as well as to those "who had fought and bled for their country." Mason agreed with Butler that the requirement would encourage speculation. And he raised what was to be a central issue in the 1790's when he declared that there was a great distinction between the original creditors and those who had purchased fraudulently from the ignorant and distressed. Gerry agreed that the soldiers and the poor and ignorant had been defrauded and that some restitution might be made to them, but he defended the "stock-jobbers" whom he said kept up the value of paper.

The Convention hurriedly backed away from so hot an issue and adopted a general formula offered by Edmund Randolph, which became the first clause of Article VI of the Constitution. It was that all debts contracted and entered into under the authority of the old Congress "shall be as valid against the United States under this Constitution, as under the Confederation." All the states except Pennsylvania voted for it.

Sherman of Connecticut was still dissatisfied. He insisted that it was necessary to connect the power to tax with the power to pay the debt, and he moved that the tax clause should be followed by a statement that it was for the payment of debts and for "defraying the expenses that shall be incurred for the common defense and general welfare." Thus Sherman proposed that Congress have the power to pay both past and future debts incurred "for the common defense and general welfare," but the Convention rejected the amendment as unnecessary. Nevertheless, the committee appointed on August 31 to consider all postponed matters reported a revision of the taxation clause in which the power to lay and collect taxes was followed by the words "to pay the debts and provide for the common defense and general welfare of the United States." Sherman's reference to future debts incurred in defense and "general welfare" was left out, and the Convention accepted the proposal without debate or dissent.

Thus the "general welfare" clause became a part of the Constitution. Was it a separate grant of power, or did it merely refer to the enumerated powers which followed it? The nationalists in the 1790's insisted that it was a separate grant, while their opponents denied it. The issue was debated for decades while Congress gradually exercised more and more power based on the welfare clause. It was able to do so because it assumed virtually unlimited power to define "welfare" and then to tax to support its definition.

Oddly enough, the assumption of state debts was never discussed after the report of the committee appointed to consider it. The reason, as Hamilton remembered it five years later, and probably correctly, was that he and Madison agreed that assumption was proper but that it would create too many obstacles to ratification, that it was "more advisable to make it a measure of administration than an article of Constitution. . . ."

The enumeration of the powers of Congress was capped, quite logically, by the "supreme law" clause. Luther

Martin had originally offered it as an alternative to the congressional veto of state laws. The Convention had agreed to his motion that the acts of Congress and United States treaties should be the "supreme law" and that the state courts should be bound thereby (and enforce them) despite state laws to the contrary. The draft constitution of August 6 subtly altered the idea. It provided that United States laws and treaties should be "supreme" over the state constitutions as well as over state laws, and that judges *in* the states should be bound by them. This meant that inferior national courts as well as state courts could have jurisdiction within the states if given the authority.

Then, on August 23, John Rutledge proposed that the United States Constitution as well as treaties and laws be the "supreme law" over state laws and constitutions. The Convention agreed without dissent or debate. With verbal changes to make it read "the supreme law of the land" and "the judges in every state" rather than "the judges in the several states," the idea became the second clause of Article VI of the Constitution.

Why had the defenders of state power and integrity not objected to a provision so sweeping in its implications? John Rutledge himself had led the fight against inferior national courts. Yet his revision of the supreme law clause meant that inferior national courts, if established and given jurisdiction, could penetrate to the farthest corner of every state and subject state laws and constitutions to the laws, the treaties, and the Constitution of the United States. Probably the answer is that the "supreme law" clause was adopted during the midst of the bitterest fight in the whole Convention: that between the North and the South over export duties, slavery, and navigation acts. So violent was it that both northerners and southerners threatened to break up the Convention by walking out. The fight was the result of certain restraints placed upon the power of Congress in the draft constitution, some of which were designed to protect the interests of the southern states.

The Restraints Upon Congressional Power. The enumerated powers in the draft constitution were followed immediately by six sections restricting the use of congressional power. The idea was an innovation of the committee of detail for only the presidential veto had been discussed by the Convention. The first related to treason. Congress was given power to punish it, but only in terms of a definition: treason was levying war against the United States or any of them, or adhering to their enemies. But no person could be convicted without the testimony of two witnesses. The definition, taken from the fourteenth-century English statute of Edward III, provided the lawyer delegates with an opportunity to display their legal learning. After much semantic hairsplitting, the Convention added the words "giving them aid and comfort" to the definition and decided that there must be two witnesses to the "same overt act" or a confession in open court before conviction for treason.

The provision that direct taxes and poll taxes be levied according to the census was agreed to after rewording. There was no objection to forbidding the United States to grant titles of nobility, a provision taken from the Articles of Confederation, and the Convention added another, also from the Articles, to the effect that no person holding office under the United States could receive presents, offices, or titles from a foreign power without the consent of Congress.

The Convention added further restrictions. The privilege of the writ of habeas corpus could not be suspended except in cases of rebellion or invasion when the public safety might require it. Congress could not pass bills of attainder or ex post facto laws. The conviction on the part of many delegates that the tax and commercial powers might be used to favor the ports of one state over another resulted in the addition of a proviso to the tax clause that all duties, imposts, and excises must be uniform throughout the United States, and to the requirement that in regulating commerce no preference was to be given to the ports of one state over another. Nor were vessels bound for one state to be required to enter, clear, or pay duties in another. Concern with financial responsibility led to adoption of a provision that no money could be drawn from the treasury "but in consequence of appropriations made by law," and to a requirement that accounts of receipts and expenditures must be published regularly. There was much talk about many of these restraints, but no fundamental disagreement.

The restraints in the draft that threatened to break up

the Convention were the result of southern distrust of the northern states. Congress was forbidden to levy export duties and to levy import duties on or prohibit the importation of "such persons" as the states might think proper to admit. Furthermore, no navigation acts could be passed without a two-thirds vote of each house of Congress. Thus, southern exports, the most valuable in the country, would not be taxed; there would be no restriction on the slave trade; and Congress would be unable to grant a monopoly of carrying southern exports to northern shipowners.

These restrictions brought the power struggle between the North and the South into the open as never before. Several northern delegates had remained bitter about the representation granted on the basis of three-fifths of the slaves. Morris and King had renewed their opposition on August 8 when Morris delivered a violent attack on the slave states. He compared the prosperity and happiness of the middle states to the "misery and poverty which overspread the barren wastes of Virginia, Maryland, and the other states having slaves." If export taxes were prohibited, and slaves imported free of duty, northern freemen would be exploited to pay the expenses of the government. The South would not pay its share but would acquire ever more representatives based on slaves. Morris moved that representation be based on free inhabitants and swore that he would rather submit to a tax to pay for all the slaves "than saddle posterity with such a Constitution." The southerners remained silent while Morris's motion was rejected.

A few days later when the Convention took up the tax power Mason counterattacked and demanded that the prohibition of export taxes be attached to the tax clause. He was supported by all the southerners except Madison, and by Ellsworth and Gerry, who thought that Congress had too much power as it was. But the debate had to be postponed because the restraints came later in the draft constitution. On August 21 the Convention reached that article and Mason stated the southern case bluntly. He subscribed to the principle that an interested majority would always exploit the minority and then asserted that the North was such a majority. Massachusetts and Connecticut joined the solid block of southern states in voting that Congress could not levy export duties. (Washington and Madison were outvoted by their colleagues on the Virginia delegation.)

The solid front of the South then broke on the slavery issue. Luther Martin proposed that there should be either a tax on the importation of slaves or a prohibition of the slave trade. He said that the counting of slaves in representation would encourage the slave trade, that slaves weakened one part of the union which the other part would be bound to protect, and that "it was inconsistent with the principles of the Revolution and dishonorable to the American character to have such a feature in the Constitution." Rutledge retorted that religion and humanity had nothing to do with the issue for "interest alone is the governing principle with nations." The true question, he declared flatly, was whether the southern states would stay in the union, and Charles Pinckney added that South Carolina would never accept the Constitution if it prohibited the slave trade.

George Mason countered with an eloquent attack on slavery and insisted that the "infernal commerce" in slaves must be stopped. And in an acid aside, he "lamented that some of our eastern brethren had from a lust of gain embarked in this nefarious traffic." General Pinckney sneered in reply that the reason Virginia was opposed to the slave trade was because she wanted a higher price for her surplus Negroes. He, too, said that a prohibition of the slave trade would exclude South Carolina from the union, and Rutledge insisted that the people of the three southernmost states would "never be such fools as to give up so important an interest." However, General Pinckney and Rutledge were willing to offer a compromise: they moved to recommit the clause so as to provide for a tax on slaves equal to that on other imports.

No one had done more to arouse southern antagonism than Gouverneur Morris, but he was always willing to make a deal. He suggested that the whole subject of export taxes, slavery, and navigation acts be sent to a committee. "These things may form a bargain among the northern and southern states."

But could they "bargain"? Butler would never agree to export taxes, while Read would not agree to commitment if export taxes were excluded. Sherman opposed a duty on slaves because it would imply that they were property. Gorham wanted to know if commitment would mean the requirement of even more votes to pass navigation acts. He warned bluntly that the "eastern states had no motive to union but a commercial one" and that they did not need the help of the southern states. Randolph swore that he would rather "risk the Constitution" than agree to the slavery clause as it stood, but he agreed that they must find some middle ground. Nevertheless, a "bargain" had to be made if the Convention were to continue, and the whole question was turned over to a committee of one from each state. The only exception was the prohibition of export taxes, which the Convention had previously agreed to.

The bargain was reported to the Convention on August 24: (1) the migration or importation of "such persons" could not be prohibited until 1800, but a tax or duty not exceeding the average rates on imports could be imposed; and (2) the requirement of a two-thirds vote to pass navigation acts would be dropped.

General Pinckney proposed at once that Congress should not interfere with the slave trade until after 1808, and Gorham, who had won on the issue of navigation acts, seconded the motion. Only Madison objected. Twenty years would produce all the mischief that could be apprehended from the importation of slaves and so long a term would be more dishonorable to the national character than to say nothing about it in the Constitution. But the Convention voted to move the date to 1808, New England lining up with the three southernmost states and Maryland to override the "no" votes of New Jersey, Delaware, Pennsylvania, and Virginia.

Gouverneur Morris proposed that to avoid ambiguity and to make it plain that this part of the Constitution was a concession to those states, the wording should be "importation of slaves into North Carolina, South Carolina, and Georgia shall not be prohibited. . . ." Mason agreed that slaves ought to be called just that, and not "such persons," but Morris withdrew his motion. Dickinson's effort to achieve the same end by pinning the restriction to those states which had not yet prohibited the importation of slaves was rejected unanimously.

The power to levy a duty on the importation of "such

persons" was again opposed by Sherman as "acknowledging men to be property." He was supported by Madison, who said he "thought it wrong to admit in the Constitution the idea that there could be property in men." Such idealism was brushed aside by King and Langdon, who "considered this as the price of the first part," and by General Pinckney, who "admitted that it was so." The Convention then agreed unanimously that Congress might impose such a tax or duty "not exceeding ten dollars for each person," which thus became the only sum of money to be mentioned anywhere in the Constitution.

The part relating to navigation acts was postponed until August 29 when Charles Pinckney threatened to disrupt the whole bargain. He proposed that the two-thirds vote for their passage be retained. He outlined the five distinct sets of commercial interests in the United States and insisted that such different interests would be a source of oppressive regulations under majority rule. "The power of regulating commerce," he said, was a "pure concession on the part of the southern states." Only Mason and Randolph supported him, Mason again insisting that the southern minority would be bound hand and foot to the "eastern" states and Randolph muttering that the Constitution already had so many odious features that he might not support it.

Ranged against Pinckney were New Englanders and South Carolinians who only a few days before had threatened to walk out of the Convention. They now blandly professed their affection for one another and their readiness to make concessions. Butler said he still thought that the interests of the eastern and the southern states were as different as those of Russia and Turkey, but that he wanted to conciliate the affections of the eastern states. Gorham again said that the eastern states would have no motive to unite unless trade were regulated by a majority vote, but he promised the South that foreign ships would not be excluded from American ports. Rutledge now assured the Convention that the power to regulate trade would not be abused, that a navigation act would cause South Carolina only temporary trouble, and that the West Indian trade (with which New England was so much concerned) must be secured for the United States. Said he grandly: "As we are laying the foundation for a great empire, we ought to take a permanent view of the subject and not look at the present moment only."

General Pinckney was the blandest of all the defenders of what was essentially a bargain between New England and South Carolina. While it was true that it was to the interest of the southern states to have no regulation of commerce, the New England states had suffered much during the war and they had shown a "liberal conduct" toward the views of South Carolina. It was proper, therefore, that no fetters be placed on the power to regulate commerce. Unblushingly, he declared that he had had prejudices against New Englanders when he came to the Convention, but that now he found them "as liberal and candid as any men whatever." Charles Pinckney's motion was smothered by such professions of good will and mutual admiration, and the rest of the bargain was agreed to unanimously. Butler of South Carolina then seized upon the harmony of the moment to propose that "if any person bound to service or labor" in one state escaped to another state he was not to be freed, but returned to his owner upon request. Everyone understood that he meant runaway slaves, and the Convention agreed unanimously to what became, with some rewording, a part of Article IV of the Constitution.

The Omission of a Bill of Rights.   The one restraint upon the power of Congress and the central government that the Convention refused to consider was a bill of rights. Such bills, defining the rights of the individual with which no government should interfere, were rooted in the Anglo-American political tradition, and Americans of the revolutionary generation were deeply attached to them. All of the revolutionary constitutions of the states included bills of rights, either as a preface or as a part of the constitutions themselves. On August 20 Charles Pinckney suggested the foundation for a national bill of rights when he proposed additional clauses providing that the liberty of the press should be "inviolably preserved," that soldiers not be quartered in houses in peacetime without the owners' consent, and that no troops be maintained in peacetime without the consent of Congress. These clauses were turned over to the committee of detail, which ignored them.

On September 12, as the Convention neared the end, Williamson and Gerry said that something should be done to preserve jury trials in civil cases. George Mason, who had written the most luminous of all the state bills of rights, urged that the Convention prepare a bill; one could, he said, be drafted in a few hours with the help of the state bills. But the ten states present unanimously rejected a motion to appoint a committee for the purpose. Two days later when Gerry and Pinckney moved that there should be a declaration asserting the liberty of the press, the only comment was Sherman's that Congress had no power over the press. The Convention then rejected the motion, seven states to four. The Constitution was thus submitted to the country without a bill of rights. Aside from the abstract principles involved, the omission was a major political error. Public opinion in the United States forced the supporters of the Constitution in several key states to promise a bill of rights as the price of ratification.

The Restraints Upon State Power. Many of the delegates were probably more concerned with placing restraints upon the state legislatures, particularly in economic matters, than with the details of government about which the small group of leaders debated so lengthily. The solution of the extreme nationalists was the congressional veto of state laws, and despite earlier defeats they proposed it once more on August 23 immediately after the "supreme law" clause was adopted. Charles Pinckney made the same motion he had in June except that the assent of two-thirds of each house would be required. Madison supported him as usual, and Wilson described the veto as "the key-stone wanted to complete the wide arch of government we are raising." Sherman replied that the supreme law clause made the veto unnecessary. Mason wanted to know if the states could not build roads or bridges without the consent of Congress and if it was to sit constantly to consider state laws. John Rutledge pronounced the funeral oration over the veto when he declared that "if nothing else, this alone would damn and ought to damn the Constitution."

The solution provided in the draft constitution was a series of four articles listing specific restraints upon state power, many of them taken directly from the Articles of Confederation. A state could not grant titles of nobility or letters of marque and reprisal or enter into any treaty, alliance, or confederation. Nor, without the consent of Congress, could a state enter into any agreement or compact with another state or with a foreign power; maintain troops or vessels in peacetime; or engage in war unless invaded or invasion were so imminent that Congress could not be consulted.

The states were required to give "full faith and credit" to the legislative acts of and judicial proceedings of other states. Citizens of each state were guaranteed all the privileges and immunities of the citizens of every other state. Persons charged with crime fleeing from one state to another must be returned at the request of the executive of the state concerned. These were all familiar restrictions, and the Convention saw little reason to argue about them.

But economic restraints were far closer to the hearts of many delegates. The draft constitution provided that the states could not coin money. And without the permission of Congress, they could not levy import duties, issue paper money, or make anything but gold and silver legal tender in the payment of debts. When the Convention took up these restrictions on August 28, delegates at once demanded that Congress have no discretion. The states should be absolutely forbidden to issue paper money or make anything but gold and silver legal tender in payment of debts. The only objection offered was that the prohibition of paper money might "rouse the most desperate opposition from its partisans." Sherman replied bluntly that this was "a favorable crisis for crushing paper money." If Congress had discretion, friends of paper money "would make every exertion to get into the legislature in order to license it." The Convention agreed heartily, only Virginia voting "no."

State laws delaying the collection of debts and altering the terms of contracts had created as much alarm as paper money. To block such laws King proposed to add a provision from the Northwest Ordinance which had been adopted the previous month by the Confederation Congress in New York. The Ordinance forbade the future northwestern states to interfere with private contracts. Morris objected that this provision was too sweeping be-

cause of the many kinds of state laws covering legal
actions. To meet this objection the Convention decided to
forbid the states to pass "retrospective" laws. However,
Dickinson consulted Blackstone's *Commentaries* and
found that ex post facto laws applied only to criminal
cases. The Convention would have to find some other way
to block state interference with private contracts. The
solution finally arrived at was the statement in the Constitution that no state could "pass any bill of attainder,
ex post facto law, or law impairing the obligation of contracts. . . ." It was this last phrase that was to provide
the principal means whereby the national courts were to
check the power of state legislatures in economic matters.

The only other economic restraint concerned import
duties. The draft provided that the states could levy such
duties if Congress consented. Madison argued that the
prohibition should be absolute and that the states should
be forbidden to lay embargoes as well. The Convention
rejected his motion, and a little later it voted that the
states could levy export duties if Congress consented.
However, it added a provision that any revenue from state
duties on imports or exports must go to the treasury of
the United States. Madison welcomed the addition for he
thought it would block state duties, but he "lamented the
complexity we were giving to the commercial system."

However, most delegates were not concerned with such
details. Their chief desire had been to abolish paper
money and state interference with private contracts, and
the Convention had done so with more enthusiasm and
harmony (and less interest in debate) than it decided any
other important issue that came before it.

The Admission of New States to the Union. The
outpouring of population across the mountains to the
westward after the treaty of peace had been followed by
demands for separation and statehood. The independent
"state" of Franklin had appeared in western North
Carolina, and the Kentuckians were ever more clamorous
to be free of Virginia's control. Far off to the northeast
Vermont maintained its independence, to the anguish of
New York and New Hampshire, and had been a political
issue in Congress for years. Meanwhile, the people of
Maine were already thinking of separation from Massachusetts. The Convention was thus forced to recognize

that new states would soon ask to join the union or else go their independent ways. But on what terms should new states enter the union?

Most of the delegates came from the older settled areas along the seacoast, and most of them shared a distrust of the men of the "back parts." The farmers in the frontier counties of the colonies had been a disruptive force before the war, and since the war the most strident demands for paper money and other "evils" had come from those same areas. Many delegates were convinced that the new western states would be dominated by the same kind of "wild men." And they frankly feared that in the future the new western states might control the government of the United States and bring evil days upon the land. Their attitude was summed up by Clymer of Pennsylvania when he said that "the encouragement of the Western Country was suicide on the part of the old States." Such men were convinced that the new states should never be admitted on equal terms.

The opposition was led by the Virginians, who had long been expansionists, and they were supported by other southern delegates who believed that new agrarian states in the southwest would add to southern weight in Congress. The committee of detail reflected the opinion of the South as opposed to that of the middle and New England states. The draft constitution provided that new states could be admitted by a two-thirds vote of Congress and, when admitted, should be "on the same terms with the original States." However, Congress might make conditions concerning the national debt then subsisting, and new states created within an existing state must also have the consent of the legislature concerned.

Gouverneur Morris continued to be the principal anti-western spokesman. He moved that the clauses providing for admission on equal terms and the public debt be eliminated. He argued that Congress should not be bound in any way, and that although he knew it was impossible to discourage the growth of the West, he did not wish to throw power into its hands. The Virginians defended the future western states, Madison insisting that they "neither would nor ought to submit to a union which degraded them from an equal rank with other states." Sherman, unlike most of his fellow New Englanders, agreed with

Madison and said that he was "for fixing an equality of privileges by the Constitution." But the opponents of the West had their way and supported Morris's motion overwhelmingly. Only Virginia and Maryland opposed it.

Morris then offered a substitute article which, with revision, became a part of Article IV of the Constitution. New states "may be" admitted by Congress, but no new states could be erected within the limits of an existing state without the consent of the legislature concerned, as well as of Congress. The first part was agreed to without objection, but the last part requiring the consent of a state legislature renewed the old fight of the landless vs. the landed states which had delayed ratification of the Articles of Confederation for nearly four years. Once more the Marylanders denounced the claims of such states as Virginia. Nothing, Luther Martin said, would more alarm the landless states than to make the consent of the large states necessary to the erection of new states within their limits.

The issue, as the delegates saw it, was quite simply whether or not a state could be dismembered without its consent. Dickinson, speaking for the small landless states, said it was improper to ask such states to guarantee the extensive claims of the large ones. Morris replied that if the purpose of the argument was the forced division of the large states, "he expected the gentlemen from these would pretty quickly leave us." Carroll of Maryland then moved to strike out the portion requiring the consent of a state and threatened that a considerable minority would oppose the Constitution if it were not done. The Pennsylvanians did not support the landless states as they had in 1776, and Wilson now declared that nothing would give greater or more justifiable alarm than the doctrine that a political society could be torn asunder without its consent. Luther Martin retorted that he wished Wilson had thought a little sooner of the value of political bodies. In the beginning, when the rights of the small states were in question, "they were phantoms, ideal beings. Now when the great states were to be affected, political societies were of a sacred nature." There was no reply Wilson could make. Martin then answered Morris by saying that the small states "will with equal firmness take their leave of the Constitution on the table."

All the efforts of the landless states to defeat Morris's

substitute article were in vain. Carroll then insisted on a provision that nothing in the Constitution should be so construed as to affect the claims of the United States to vacant lands ceded by the treaty of peace, and he frankly admitted he had in mind lands claimed by some of the states. Wilson and Madison thought it best to say nothing in the Constitution. However, Madison suggested that to make the proviso "neutral" it should also state that the claims of the states were not to be affected. Morris then proposed what became the last clause of section 3 of Article IV of the Constitution: Congress should have power to dispose of and make all rules and regulations for the territory and other property of the United States, but nothing in the Constitution should "be so construed as to prejudice any claims of the United States or of any particular state."

Meanwhile, a slight but significant change provided for the admission of Vermont. New York claimed that Vermont was within its "limits," and the Convention had agreed that no state could be created within the limits of a state without the consent of its legislature. Sherman and Johnson of Connecticut offered various suggestions, but the adept Morris had a simple solution: substitute the word "jurisdiction" for the word "limits." The Convention agreed. Vermont might be within the "limits" of New York, but the Vermonters had seen to it that New York had no "jurisdiction."

Congress was therefore left with unlimited discretion to impose conditions upon new states, but the hope of the majority in the Convention that the old states could retain their dominant position was doomed. Some of the delegates lived long enough to be convinced that their fears of western expansion in 1787 had been fully justified.

The States, Congress, and the Amending Process. The delegates agreed that the Constitution would need amending in the future. The draft of August 6 proposed that whenever two-thirds of the state legislatures requested an amendment, Congress must call a convention to consider it. The initiative was thus left entirely to the states and the final decision to a convention. The Convention accepted the provision. This satisfied those who feared a too-powerful central government, but not the nationalists.

The nationalists got their chance a few days later when

Gerry moved reconsideration. He feared that two-thirds of the states might subvert the state constitutions. Hamilton, who had returned for the last few days of the Convention, seconded the motion, but for a quite different reason. He declared that the states would never request a convention except to increase their own power, and then proposed that Congress have the power to call a convention whenever two-thirds of each house agreed. Sherman combined the two ideas by moving that Congress as well as the state legislatures could propose amendments.

Madison and Hamilton then presented the nationalist counter-proposal which would give control to Congress, avoid national conventions in the future, and make the amending process more complex. Congress could propose amendments by a two-thirds vote of each house, or whenever two-thirds of the state legislatures requested them, but they must be ratified either by three-fourths of the state legislatures or by state conventions, and Congress would decide which. The Convention agreed, 9-1.

At the very end the states righters again raised the issue by demanding restrictions on the amending process. On September 15 Sherman asserted that three-fourths of the states could do "fatal things" to "particular states," even abolish them entirely. George Mason insisted that the amending process was dangerous. It gave Congress ultimate control, and no amendment could ever be "obtained by the people" if the government became oppressive, as he believed it would.

Morris, for the nationalists, offered a concession: he moved to restore the provision that two-thirds of the state legislatures could require Congress to call a convention. Madison was dubious, but the Convention agreed unanimously. However, men like Sherman were not satisfied. Sherman moved that a state should not be deprived by amendments of control of its internal police or its equality in the senate without its consent. The precedent for restricting the amending process had been set on September 10. John Rutledge, ever alert to defend the slave interest, had secured a proviso that until 1808 no amendment could interfere with the slave trade or the apportionment of direct and poll taxes. Sherman's motion was rejected, for the great majority of the Convention was convinced that the new government should interfere in the internal affairs of the states. But equality in the senate was another matter, and Morris moved that it be guaranteed. "This motion," reported Madison, "being dictated by the circulating murmurs of the small states, was agreed to without debate, no one opposing it, or on the question saying no."

Immediately after this vote George Mason moved that until 1808 a two-thirds majority be required to pass navigation acts. He asserted that a simple majority would enable a few rich merchants of Boston, New York, and Philadelphia "to monopolize the staples of the southern states and reduce their value perhaps fifty per cent." The Convention, committed to the hard-won compromise of the previous month, refused to agree.

Although the nationalists were forced to make concessions, they had achieved their aim of transferring control of the amending process from the states to Congress. The states were left with a passive role: they must await the submission of amendments to them. They had lost their power to propose amendments, and they have never used their right to request a constitutional convention.

The States, the Confederation Congress, and Ratification. Even before the Convention met, some of the nationalist leaders were convinced that a new constitution could never be ratified except by state conventions. During the early debates they had won out in repeated votes, and the draft of August 6 accepted the fact. During the debate that followed, however, Gouverneur Morris broke ranks with his fellow nationalists by proposing that the states be allowed to ratify in any way they pleased. His motive, he said, was to make ratification easier, but he desisted when King declared flatly that this method would be "equivalent to giving up the business altogether." Madison added a defense of the convention method, pointing out that since the power of the central government would be taken from the state governments, the state legislatures would be less likely to ratify than conventions composed, in part at least, of other men. "The people," he said, "were in fact the fountain of all power, and by resorting to them, all difficulties were got over." Men like Martin and Carroll, who demanded ratification by state legislatures, and unanimous ratification at that, were overridden as they had been before. The final decision was for ratification by state conventions.

The draft of August 6, however, did not specify the number of states necessary to ratify, and when that question was taken up on August 30 James Wilson at once proposed seven, a simple majority. The other extreme was represented by Carroll of Maryland, who argued that since all 13 states had been required to ratify the Articles of Confederation, all 13 must agree to dissolve it. The Convention finally accepted Randolph's proposal that nine states, the "number made familiar by the constitution of the existing Congress," should be enough. The Convention agreed also to King's practical amendment that the operation of the new government should be confined to the states actually ratifying it.

A far thornier question was the role to be played by the Confederation Congress. The draft of August 6 provided that the new Constitution must be approved by Congress before submission to the states. As soon as the article was considered, the nationalists moved to strike it out. The Convention agreed, 8-3. Morris and Pinckney then moved a revised article which merely required that the Constitution be laid before Congress and then submitted to a convention chosen in each state at the direction of its legislature. Morris said conventions should be called speedily to "prevent enemies to the plan from giving it the go by." The first reaction of the people would be favorable, but in time state officers and those interested in state governments would "intrigue and turn the popular current against it."

The states righters and other opponents of various parts of the document now made a stand. Luther Martin declared that Morris was right and that the people would never ratify the Constitution "unless hurried into it by surprise." Gerry agreed with Martin and talked of the impropriety of destroying the Confederation without the unanimous consent of the parties to it. George Mason swore that "he would sooner chop off his right hand than put it to the Constitution as it now stands," and he supported Edmund Randolph's idea that the state ratifying conventions should be free to propose amendments for consideration by another convention. When Mason and Gerry moved to postpone the whole article, Morris angrily agreed. He had long wished for another convention "that will have the firmness to provide a vigorous government, which we are afraid to do." However, the Convention rejected the motion and once more agreed that congressional approval should not be required.

Gerry returned to the attack on September 10. He insisted that Congress must approve, and he again objected to abolishing the Confederation "with so little scruple or formality." Surprisingly, he had the support of Alexander Hamilton. In the early days of the Convention Hamilton had made it clear that he had little respect for the states or for the old Congress, but he now declared that approval by Congress was a "necessary ingredient in the transaction." Furthermore, it would be wrong to allow nine states to "institute a new government on the ruins of the existing one."

At first the other nationalists replied that it was more respectful to submit the Constitution to Congress than to require its approval, which would demand an act inconsistent with its authority under the Articles of Confederation. But the Convention voted to reconsider, and Hamilton then moved that Congress approve the Constitution before it was sent to the states. He suggested also that in calling a convention a state legislature should provide that if the convention ratified the Constitution, it should be binding on the state. He would also allow the state conventions to decide whether or not ratification by nine states would be sufficient.

The proposal was welcomed by the states-rights federalist group, but the other nationalists would have none of it. James Wilson declared that the time had come to speak freely: it was worse than folly to rely upon agreement by the Rhode Island members of Congress and it was not "safe" to require the approval of Congress. After laboring hard for four or five months "we are ourselves at the close throwing insuperable obstacles in the way of its success." King echoed him, as did Clymer and Rutledge. The Convention then rejected Hamilton's motion and once more agreed not to ask the approval of Congress.

In the end, much of this hotly debated question was omitted from the Constitution. The final article simply stated that ratification by the conventions of nine states would be sufficient to establish the Constitution among the states ratifying it. The delegates then resolved that the Constitution should be laid before Congress, and that it was the opinion of the Convention that the Constitution should thereafter be submitted to state ratifying conventions.

— 11 —

THE SENATE, THE PRESIDENCY, AND THE JUDICIARY

Between August 23 and 28 the delegates again debated three major parts of the Constitution, and at the end they seemed no nearer agreement than ever over the senate and the presidency. However, they did agree on the essentials of the judiciary.

The Senate. Most of the nationalists conceived of the senate as a body which would represent stability and property, as opposed to the house of representatives, which, because it represented "the people," would inevitably be unstable and inclined to attack property rights. This was the classical theory in which they believed, but their aims had been shattered by political reality. The small states and those delegates who believed in a "federal" as opposed to a "national" government had forced adoption of the compromise which meant that the states would be represented in the senate as states, and with equal voting power.

At the same time, the distrust of executive power, a heritage of the revolutionary debate of 1776, had produced the assignment of wide powers to the senate, in addition to its legislative function. Article IX of the draft constitution gave the senate the power to make treaties, appoint supreme court judges and ambassadors, and establish courts to settle disputes between states over territory and disputes arising from conflicting land grants by two or more states. These powers assigned to the senate were exercised by Congress under the Articles of Confederation.

Most of the nationalist leaders were distrustful of legislative power, whether state or national, and they had made it clear that they wanted a powerful executive who would represent the "monarchical" principle which they believed was necessary in any "balanced" government. Gouverneur Morris now attacked the appointive power given the senate, charging that it was too large a body to be responsible. Madison declared that the treaty-making power should be given the president because the senate now represented the states. Gorham was positive that if Congress had anything whatever to do with treaties, it would be corrupted by foreign ambassadors.

However, the Convention quickly agreed to eliminate the senate's power to establish courts, most delegates agreeing that the national judiciary should decide disputes over land. Even so, some delegates were worried that judges, like legislators, would be easily corrupted if their interests or those of their states were involved. Here, as throughout the Convention, the members made clear their conviction that men in public office would use their positions to further their private interests unless checked in some manner. There was nothing unusual about this for it was a common assumption among the educated men of the eighteenth century.

The Presidency. The Convention differed even more strenuously about the presidency than about the senate. The draft constitution provided that the executive should be a single person called "The President of the United States of America," to be elected by Congress for seven years and ineligible for a second term. The president would report on the "state of the union," execute the laws, commission officers of the United States and appoint officials not otherwise provided for in the Constitution, grant reprieves and pardons, and be commander in chief of the army and navy and of the militia of the states. He would be removable from office after impeachment by the house of representatives for treason, bribery, or corruption and conviction in the supreme court. In case of the president's removal, death, or disability, the president of the senate would act as president until a successor was chosen or the disability removed.

The Convention agreed on the title, but the fight between the large and small states broke out again when

Rutledge moved that the president be elected by a joint ballot of the two houses. Large-state delegates argued that it would be "reasonable" to give their states a greater share in the election, while most of the small-state group insisted on a separate ballot which would give the senate equal power with the house. Carroll's motion that the president be elected "by the people" was rejected without discussion. The Convention voted for a joint ballot, 7-4, and then rejected a small-state motion that each state have one vote on the joint ballot.

This argument was really a side issue so far as most of the nationalists were concerned. They wanted a president free from congressional control and with power to check Congress. Therefore, most of them opposed election by Congress, but they had never been able to agree on an alternative method. Gouverneur Morris again charged that election by Congress would lead to "legislative tyranny," corruption, and endless intrigue. On the other hand, men such as Mason, Randolph, Sherman, and Dickinson—men who believed in the revolutionary theory and practice of a supreme legislature—were opposed to a powerful executive. Morris's motion that electors chosen by the people of the states should elect the president was rejected, 6-5, and the Convention split evenly when asked to vote on Morris's proposal "as an abstract question." Then it once more delayed decision by a postponement.

The delegates made far more progress in agreeing upon the duties and powers of the president. Some changes were slight although the delegates thought them of great importance. They changed "may" recommend measures to "shall" recommend, "to make it the duty of the president to recommend, and thence prevent umbrage or cavil at his doing it." When Sherman declared that the power to "appoint officers" might enable the president to create an army and "set up an absolute government," Madison moved and the Convention agreed to substitute "offices" for "officers." But Dickinson insisted on still more precision. He said the president should have power to fill those offices created by the Constitution and not otherwise provided for, and those thereafter created by law. The Convention agreed, but it rejected a motion by Dickinson and Randolph to give Congress power to allow state governors or legislatures to fill certain offices. The nationalists would have none of this states rights proposal. As Morris said, it would enable the states to say "you shall be viceroys, but we will be viceroys over you."

Sherman met defeat when he tried to join the senate with the president in exercising the pardoning power, but the Convention agreed that pardons should not apply in cases of impeachment. Sherman was alarmed, too, as he had been before, about the power of the central government over the militia. The Convention accepted his motion that the president be commander in chief of state militia only when it was in service of the United States.

The nationalists objected to removal of the president after impeachment by the house and conviction by the supreme court, with the president of the senate to serve as his successor. Morris objected that the court would be the wrong body to try a president if the chief justice were to be a member of the proposed privy council. Madison predicted that the senate might delay electing a successor to "carry points" while the veto power was in the hands of its presiding officer. Williamson suggested that Congress ought to provide for the succession, but then moved postponement of the debate. The Convention agreed unanimously. Meanwhile, in seconding the motion, John Dickinson asked a question which neither the Convention nor the Constitution answered, and which has not been answered to this day: "what is the extent of the term 'disability,' and who is to be the judge of it?"

The Judiciary.   The Convention then turned to the judiciary. It had agreed upon a supreme court from the start, and most delegates assumed that it would rule upon the constitutionality of state and national laws. On July 18 the Convention had accepted Madison's proposal of the broadest possible jurisdiction: "to all cases arising under the national laws and to such other questions as may involve the national peace and harmony."

The draft constitution ignored this broad grant and stated the role of the supreme court in specific detail. The "judicial power of the United States" would consist of one supreme court and such inferior courts as Congress might establish, with judges holding office during good behavior. The original jurisdiction of the supreme court would extend to cases of impeachment, those affecting ambassadors and other foreign officials, and controversies between two or more states (except those involving territory or jurisdiction). The court's appellate jurisdiction (with such regulations and exceptions as Congress might make) would extend to cases arising under the laws of the United States; to all cases of admiralty and maritime jurisdiction; and to controversies between two or more states, between citizens of different states, and between a state or its citizens and a foreign state or its citizens. However, Congress could assign any part of the jurisdiction, except the trial of the president, to such inferior courts as it might establish.

The Convention at once amended the first section to read that "the judicial power of the United States both in law and equity shall be vested in one supreme court. . . ." It postponed a decision on the power to try impeachments because of disagreement over the presidency. The Convention then greatly extended the power of the supreme court. It accepted Doctor Johnson's motion that jurisdiction be extended to cases arising under the Constitution as well as under the laws of the United States. Madison warned that it would be going too far to extend the jurisdiction to all cases arising under the Constitution; he suggested that it be limited to cases of a "judiciary nature." Madison meant that the court should not be asked to decide upon constitutional questions except when a case involving a disputed constitutional point was actually before it. The Convention accepted Johnson's motion with the understanding that the jurisdiction "was constructively limited to cases of a judiciary nature." Jurisdiction over treaties made or to be made was added without objection.

A few days before, the senate had been stripped of its power to erect courts to settle land disputes. Sherman now moved to give the court jurisdiction in cases between "citizens of the same state claiming lands under grants of different states." His purpose was to take care of such matters as the rival land grants of Connecticut and Pennsylvania within the Wyoming Valley of the latter state, and those of New York and New Hampshire within Vermont.

After the question was raised, the Convention voted

that the court's appellate jurisdiction should extend to matters of fact as well as law. It agreed that the appellate jurisdiction should be regulated by Congress, but rejected an attempt to allow Congress to direct the exercise of judicial power. The Convention then eliminated the provision that Congress might assign any part of the supreme court's jurisdiction to inferior courts.

According to the draft constitution, all criminal offenses must be tried by juries in the states where they occurred. The Convention added a provision to insure jury trials for crimes committed outside of a state. Two or three delegates raised the question of guaranteeing jury trials in civil cases, but they were ignored. The opponents of the Constitution made much of the omission in the struggle over ratification, and demanded that such a guarantee be included in a bill of rights.

By August 28 the Convention had agreed on all the essentials of the judiciary as it appeared in the final draft of the Constitution, and it did so with remarkably little disagreement. Neither then nor later did the delegates suggest that the supreme court be expressly authorized to rule on the constitutionality of state and national laws. They took it for granted that it should and would do so.

— 12 —

THE COMPLETION OF THE CONSTITUTION

The Achievement of the Committee on Unfinished Parts. August 31 the Convention turned a variety of postponed and bitterly contested issues over to a committee of one from each state. It began reporting back the next day, offering verbal changes and new formulations to settle long-standing disputes. Then on September 4 it proposed, in a complex set of compromises, a striking alteration in the internal power structure of the central government itself. The three leading large-state nationalists on the committee—Madison, King, and Morris —gained much, but they had to pay a price for the support of the small states, which, it was assumed, would control the senate. As Madison explained it, certain delegates had set great store on the "privilege" of giving exclusive control of money bills to the house of representatives. In the committee the members from the small states, and some from the large states who "wished a high mounted government," combined to make "that privilege the price of arrangements in the Constitution favorable to the small states, and to the elevation of the government."

The nationalist leaders had opposed exclusive control of money bills by the house, while men like Gerry, Mason, and Randolph had fought vigorously for it. The Convention had voted to give the senate equal power, but the issue remained unsettled. As a compromise, the committee proposed that all revenue bills originate in the house, but be subject to alteration and amendment by the senate. The next part of the compromise involved the presidency and the senate. The nationalists, opposed to the treaty-making and appointing power of the senate, managed to assign those powers to the president, but as a concession to the small states they had to agree that the senate must approve appointments, and as a concession to the southern states, that two-thirds of the senators present must ratify treaties. In addition, the power to try impeachments of the president was transferred from the supreme court to the senate, the argument being that the judges should not try the official who appointed them to office.

Madison, King, and Morris were the leading opponents of congressional election of the president and of a single term in office. They believed that a powerful executive, able to act as a brake on legislative irresponsibility, could never be established under such conditions. They won a partial victory in the committee, for it proposed that the president be elected by electors chosen in the states in any way their legislatures might direct. The states would have as many electors as they had members of Congress. The electors would meet in each state and vote for two men, one of whom could not be an inhabitant of the state. The votes would be sent to the senate to be counted. The man with a majority of the electoral votes would be president and the one with the next highest number, vice-president. In case of a tie, the senate would choose between the two candidates, and if no man had a majority it would elect a president from among the five highest on the list. Finally, the president would have a four-year term and be eligible for re-election. He must be a natural-born citizen of the United States, or a citizen at the time of the adoption of the Constitution, and a resident for 14 years. He would be removable for treason or bribery after impeachment by the house and conviction by a two-thirds vote of the senate.

In the eyes of most members of the Convention, the new method freed the president from election by Congress only in the first instance. They agreed that 19 times out of 20 the senate would have to decide because they were convinced that in so vast a country very few men would ever become well enough known to win a majority of electoral votes. An exception, of course, was George Washington, whom everyone assumed would be the first president. The delegates also looked upon the method as yet another compromise between the large and small states. They assumed that the large states would nominate the candidates, but that the small states in the senate would elect the president.

The compromise package threatened another endless debate. Morris and Sherman allied to defend the bargain that had been made, while nationalists like Pinckney and Rutledge joined Mason, Randolph, Dickinson, and Gerry in opposition to many parts of it. Madison for once seemed of two minds, although he clung to the conviction that a "primary object" was to prevent Congress from playing any role in electing the president. A few like Randolph and Rutledge continued to argue that Congress should elect, but most of the delegates accepted the idea of electors, a method suggested several times during the previous months.

Morris supported the plan. He repeated his old arguments about the "indispensable necessity" of an executive independent of the legislature and of the dangers of cabal and corruption. Still another reason for it, he said, was that some people even wanted "an immediate choice by the people." Over and over again he insisted that the senate would seldom elect a president, but most of the Convention disagreed.

Some opponents of the plan swore that the president would be a mere creature of the senate; others, that he would combine with it to establish a "dangerous aristocracy." Several agreed with Mason that the senate would have too much power and that it might combine with the president to "subvert" the Constitution. These men suggested that the house of representatives, not the senate, should elect the president in case of a tie vote or when no candidate had a majority. When Wilson and Dickinson first moved this alternative, the Convention rejected it. Madison then moved that any candidate who got one-third of the electoral vote should be president. The Convention rejected this proposal overwhelmingly, and various other suggestions as well. At the end of the day McHenry commented that the Convention had spent the greatest part of the time in "desultory conversation. . . ."

On September 6 the Convention began by agreeing that no national legislator or officeholder could be an elector. Gerry then moved that the house of representatives elect the president for a second term if he did not receive a majority of electoral votes, a device which would free him from dependence on the senate for continuance in office. The suggestion won considerable support, but Sherman, ever alert to guard the interest of the small states, proposed that if the house elected, it should vote by states. Wilson then railed against the vast power of the senate, and Hamilton declared that under the old system the president "was a monster elected for seven years." He supported Madison's idea that the highest number of electoral votes, whether a majority or not, should be enough to elect.

After a flurry of motions, the Convention suddenly came to an agreement. Williamson of North Carolina proposed that the president be elected by "the legislature voting *by states* and not *per capita*." Sherman then moved that whenever no candidate had a majority, the house should immediately choose a president by ballot, "the members from each state having one vote." Mason liked the idea because it lessened the aristocratic influence of the senate, and the motion passed with only Delaware dissenting.

Madison at once raised the question of what should constitute a quorum for the purposes of electing a president, and the result was an amendment requiring representatives of two-thirds of the states to be present. The next day Gerry moved that a majority of the states must vote for a candidate before he could be elected, and Madison supported him heartily. The Convention agreed, and thus ended its longest, weariest, and most confusing debate. As James Wilson said at one point: "It is in truth the most difficult of all on which we have had to decide." The irony of it was that the delegates were almost completely wrong in one of their basic assumptions, for only twice since 1789 has the house of representatives ever elected a president.

While the Convention debated the presidency much of the time between September 4 and 8, it also managed to agree on other parts of the committee report. Decision on the control of money bills had been postponed at the insistence of Morris, who wanted to see what action the Convention would take on other parts of the compromise. On September 8 the Convention gave the senate the right to share in money legislation by adopting the language of the Massachusetts Constitution: the senate "may propose or concur with amendments as in other bills." Madison noted that "this was a conciliatory vote, the effect of the compromise formerly alluded to."

The committee had provided for a vice-president, an official found in some of the states, but one which had not been discussed by the Convention. Most of the delegates seemed to feel that a vice-president would be useless except as a possible successor to the president, although a few like Gerry and Mason professed to see danger in having him preside over the senate. However, the Convention agreed with Sherman who said that if the vice-president did not so preside, "he would be without employment. . . ."

The location of the power of appointment excited far more debate, for the delegates were convinced that whatever agency appointed men to office would acquire a disproportionate amount of strength within the government. The nationalist leaders had managed to transfer the power from the senate to the president, but they had been forced to agree that the senate must ratify appointments. This did not satisfy men like Mason, who objected to legislative participation in appointments but declared it was too dangerous a power to trust to the president. He proposed that the president have a council and charged that the omission of one was "an experiment on which the most despotic governments have never ventured." At the other extreme were men like Wilson, who argued that the president's power of appointment should not be checked by the senate.

The Convention rejected a council but agreed that the president could require written opinions from the heads of executive departments and thus casually provided the only constitutional basis for the president's cabinet. It then voted that the president should appoint ambassadors, judges, and other officials not provided for in the Constitution. It also adopted an amendment allowing the president to fill vacancies during recesses of the senate, with tenure to run until the end of its next session. This made it possible for presidents, if they so chose, to ignore the will of the senate from time to time.

When the Convention took up the question of impeachment, Mason at once insisted that the grounds of treason and bribery were too limited. He declared that many great and dangerous offenses, even attempts to subvert the Constitution, might not be covered by the definition of treason provided in the draft. He moved to add "maladministration" as a basis for impeachment, but when Madison objected that so vague a term would mean tenure at the pleasure of the senate, Mason substituted "other high crimes and misdemeanors against the state." Madison and Pinckney then made a last-minute effort to return trials of impeachment to the supreme court, using the old argument that the president would be too dependent on the legislature. Morris agreed that "legislative tyranny [was] the great danger to be apprehended," but warned that the supreme court was so small that it "might be warped or corrupted." The delegates found this a reasonable proposition and rejected Madison's motion.

However, they agreed that "high crimes and misdemeanors" should be added to the grounds for impeachment.

Treaty-Making Power.   The debate on the treaty-
making power was short but tense. The nationalist leaders had won a victory in transferring it from the senate
to the president. The committee also proposed that the
senate must ratify treaties, and James Wilson even wanted
the house to ratify as well, since treaties would have the
force of law. The nationalist leaders divided, however,
as to the number of senators necessary, a disagreement
revealing the continuing split between the North and the
South. Most northerners insisted that a simple majority
was enough, while southern nationalists such as Madison
insisted upon a two-thirds majority, and considered even
that too small. What was at stake were the conflicting
interests of the northern merchants and the southern
planters. The delegates retained vivid memories of the
North-South fight over the Jay-Gardoqui treaty of the
previous year. Jay had given up American claims to a
right to navigate the Mississippi River for a period of
years in return for commercial privileges in Spanish
ports. The southerners had been outraged, and the five
southern states in Congress had defeated the treaty because under the Articles of Confederation nine states
must ratify.

The committee, to satisfy the southerners, proposed
that two-thirds of the senators present must ratify treaties.
When the Convention took up the proposal, Madison
offered a partial compromise by moving that a simple
majority be enough to ratify peace treaties. The Convention agreed, and Madison then proposed that two-
thirds of the senate be empowered to make peace treaties
without the consent of the president. He argued that a
president would acquire so much power during a war
that he might be unwilling to make peace. He was supported by Butler of South Carolina, who cited examples
from history to demonstrate that such a provision was
"a necessary security against ambitious and corrupt
presidents."

The Convention then voted to reconsider the whole
treaty provision, and the next day Wilson once more
argued for a simple majority to ratify. Gerry, on the

other hand, charged that even a two-thirds majority was too small and predicted darkly that the senate would be corrupted by foreign influence. Sherman was afraid that even the Treaty of 1783 would be subverted and wanted some guarantee against such an event. Some of the realities behind the debate were set forth by Gouverneur Morris. He asserted that unless a simple majority were required for peace treaties, Congress would be unwilling to make war for the fisheries and the Mississippi, "the two great objects of the union." In the end, the Convention rejected a variety of motions to make ratification even more difficult, and then accepted the original committee report: two-thirds of the senators present must ratify all treaties.

The Final Draft of the Constitution. By Saturday, September 8, the delegates were impatient with further delay, and they elected a committee of five "to revise the style of and arrange the articles which had been agreed to by the house." The 23 articles adopted during the month-long debate on the draft constitution of August 6 were turned over to King, Johnson, Hamilton, Morris, and Madison as a "committee of style."

While the Convention awaited the committee's report, it continued to debate certain issues. It altered the amending and ratifying process, as we have seen. It also changed the number of votes necessary to override a presidential veto. Earlier, when the Convention had voted that Congress should elect the president, a three-fourths vote of each house had been required. Williamson of North Carolina, who had made the earlier motion, now moved that two-thirds of each house should be enough. The Convention agreed, 6-4, despite bitter-end opposition from the nationalist leaders. They objected to any lessening of presidential power and expounded once more on the danger of legislative tyranny and usurpation.

The Convention also yielded to a repeated southern demand for the right to levy export taxes to pay the costs of the inspection laws used to maintain the quality of southern exports. Delegates from such states as New Jersey clamored that they would be exploited by their neighbors if the states were given this power. Madison replied that "the jurisdiction of the supreme court must be the source of redress," but, he added plaintively, the only real solution was the congressional veto of state legislation. The Convention finally agreed that the states could tax exports for the purpose demanded, after giving Congress the power to control such legislation in case of abuse.

The Constitution, in virtually final form, is reputedly the work of Gouverneur Morris. It was submitted to the Convention on Wednesday, September 12, and the next day printed copies were placed in the hands of the delegates. The committee of style had reduced the 23 articles to 7, rearranged many provisions, and revised the language in the direction of clarity and precision. As with the Virginia Resolutions of May 29, the report of June 13 on those resolutions, and the draft constitution of August 6, the delegates went through the Constitution article by article. They started on Thursday and had completed the task by Saturday afternoon, September 15. Some "verbal alterations" were made, but even more were rejected, for as Madison noted at one point, "a number of members being very impatient," they called for the question. A few changes were made. The Convention dropped the provision that Congress should elect the treasurer of the United States, thus leaving the appointment to the president. Mason and Gerry insisted on the annual publication of government income and expenses, while Madison argued that such reports should be published "from time to time." The Convention combined the extremes by voting that there should be a "regular" publication of income and expenses "from time to time."

Many important additional powers—to dig canals, grant charters of incorporation, and establish a university —were proposed, but the Convention rejected these and others one by one. The only significant change agreed upon during the last working day was to add a restriction demanded by the small states: the amending process could not be used to deprive the states of their equality in the senate.

The Convention was now ready to vote on the Constitution, but before it did so Edmund Randolph restated his objections and declared that he would not sign unless the delegates agreed to a second convention to consider amendments proposed by the state ratifying conventions. Mason backed up Randolph and stated that he, too, would refuse to sign unless a second convention were called. Elbridge Gerry likewise voiced his objections and announced that he would not sign. Thereupon the states present rejected Randolph's proposal unanimously, and equally unanimously agreed to the Constitution and ordered it engrossed. The Convention then adjourned to Monday, September 17.

When the engrossed Constitution was laid before the Convention on Monday morning, James Wilson read a long conciliatory speech written by Franklin. Franklin agreed that the Constitution had many faults, but he doubted that another Convention could produce a better one. He appealed for unanimity in signing it and offered an "ambiguous form" prepared by Gouverneur Morris "to gain the dissenting members, and put into the hands of Doctor Franklin that it might have the better chance of success." The proposal read: "Done in Convention, by the unanimous consent of *the States* present the 17th. of Sepr.&c—In Witness whereof we have hereunto subscribed our names." McHenry acidly described the speech as "plain, insinuating, persuasive—and in any event of the system, guarded the Doctor's fame."

As soon as Wilson finished reading, Gorham of Massachusetts proposed an important change. Several attempts had been made to increase the number of representatives allotted to this or that state, but they had always been rejected. Gorham now moved, "for the purpose of lessening objections to the Constitution," that there should be one representative for every 30,000 of population, instead of one for every 40,000. King and Carroll seconded the motion, and when Washington rose to put the question he made his only speech in the Convention. He supported the proposal because "it was much to be desired that the objections to the plan recommended might be made as few as possible," and because he had always believed that "the smallness of the proportion of representatives" was "among the exceptionable parts of the plan. . . ." Gorham's motion was adopted at once and without dissent.

The states then agreed unanimously to the engrossed Constitution (*see Reading No. 4*), whereupon the delegates began quibbling about Franklin's "ambiguous form."

Morris explained that it "related only to the fact that the states present were unanimous." He said that he, too, had objections, but would abide by the majority will and take the Constitution with all its faults. The great question was "shall there be a national government or not?" If not, there would be anarchy. Hamilton, too, appealed for unanimity in signing, for a few "characters of consequence" might "do infinite mischief" by refusing. "No man's ideas were more remote from the plan than his own were known to be," but it was possible to choose between anarchy and convulsion on one side and the "chance of good" on the other.

Morris's superficial cleverness did not deceive Randolph. Signing the proposed form would be the same as signing the Constitution, and he would sign neither, although he might support the Constitution if circumstances warranted. General Pinckney scoffed at the "ambiguity" of the form which would win no converts. The Convention should be candid and not leave the meaning of the signers in doubt. He would sign the Constitution and would work for it with all his influence.

Gerry was no more impressed than Randolph. Where Morris and Hamilton saw anarchy if the Constitution were not adopted, he saw the threat of civil war if it were submitted to the people in its present form. There were two parties in Massachusetts, "one devoted to democracy, the worst he thought of all political evils, the other as violent in the opposite extreme." Chaos might result from a collision of the two parties over the Constitution.

The Convention finally agreed to the form unanimously, except for South Carolina, whose vote was divided because General Pinckney and Butler voted against the equivocation in the form. All that remained was to sign, but before this could be done King raised the question of what to do with the records of the Convention. He felt they should either be destroyed or placed in Washington's hands because if made public, bad use would be made of them by opponents of the Constitution. Wilson agreed, and said they should be retained in order to contradict any false suggestions that might be propagated. The Convention then voted to give the records to Washington, and the delegates were at last ready to sign.

As they finished, Benjamin Franklin made the last statement recorded by James Madison. Franklin remarked to members sitting near him that he was now convinced that the painting of the sun over the President's chair "is a rising and not a setting sun." Madison then ended his long chronicle of three and a half months of debate prosaically:

> The Constitution being signed by all the members except Mr. Randolph, Mr. Mason, and Mr. Gerry, who declined giving it the sanction of their names, the Convention dissolved itself by an adjournment *sine die.*

— 13 —

THE MAJOR ISSUES IN THE PUBLIC DEBATE

The Confederation Congress and the Constitution. Three days after the Convention ended, the Constitution was laid before Congress, and King, Gorham, Madison, and others who were also members of Congress hastened to New York. They urged Congress to send the Constitution to the states with its positive approval and with an exhortation to ratify as soon as possible. Richard Henry Lee, who had refused to go to the Convention because as a member of Congress he would have to consider the work of the Convention, led Nathan Dane of Massachusetts and Melancthon Smith of New York in opposition. Lee described the supporters of the Constitution as a "coalition of monarchy men, military men, aristocrats, and drones whose noise, impudence, and zeal" exceeded belief. Lee and his small minority argued that members of Congress could not approve a document "which had for its object the subversion of the constitution under which they acted." Such opposition was so effective that in order to achieve "unanimity," Congress sent the Constitution to the states without approval or disapproval—a "bare transmission," Madison called it.

In the course of the three-day debate the supporters of

the Constitution admitted that Congress had the right to offer amendments. Lee thereupon offered a bill of rights and some specific amendments. His preamble voiced once more the distrust of officeholders which had been so much a part of the political thinking of 1776: universal experience proved that "the most express declarations and reservations are necessary to protect the just rights and liberty of mankind from the silent, powerful, and ever active conspiracy of those who govern. . . ." His "bill of rights" contained many of the ideas later included in the first ten amendments.

Lee also proposed to change certain structural details. The president would have a privy council to give advice which would be a matter of public record. In order to avoid mingling legislative and executive power, the council rather than the senate would join with the president in making appointments. The vice-presidency would be abolished for the same reason. Trials by juries in the vicinity in both civil and criminal cases would be guaranteed. People could not be called from "their own country" in disputes with citizens of other states and with foreigners because the distance and expense involved would force them to submit to ill-founded demands. The number of representatives in the house, "where the popular interest must chiefly depend for protection," would be increased, as would the number of votes required to pass laws. Congress rejected the proposals, but Lee had, in effect, provided a part of the platform on which the opponents of the Constitution were to stand.

The debate over ratification of the Constitution took place in mass meetings, private meetings, legislatures, and finally, in the state conventions. Such discussions were accompanied by a newspaper and pamphlet debate which equaled in intensity, quality, and quantity the debate immediately preceding the Declaration of Independence. Newspaper publications ranged from scurrilous squibs, "recipes," and doggerel poetry to the high level of Richard Henry Lee's *Letters from the Federal Farmer* in opposition to, and *The Federalist* in support of, ratification. There was an enormous amount of quibbling about this, that, and the other detail of the Constitution, but three major areas of dispute stand out above all others. These concerned (1) the very nature of the new government itself; (2) the state of the economy and its relationship to the central government; and (3) the question of whether a bill of rights should be added to the new Constitution.

The Debate over the Nature of the Central Government. Five days before the Convention finished its work, the *Pennsylvania Gazette* declared that "the former distinction of the citizens of America . . . into Whigs and Tories should be lost in the more important distinction of Federal and Antifederal men. The former are the friends of liberty and independence; the latter are the enemies of liberty, and the secret abettors of the interests of Great Britain." The supporters of the Constitution thus began their campaign for ratification by mislabelling the opposition and slurring its patriotism.

Ever since then the label of Anti-Federalist has been applied to such men as Richard Henry Lee, Patrick Henry, George Mason, George Clinton, and Elbridge Gerry, although in fact they were true "federalists," as both they and the men of the Convention well knew. They believed that a "federal" rather than a "national" constitution was better suited to so huge a country with such a variety of conflicting interests. Samuel Adams stated their position clearly after reading the new Constitution: "I confess as I enter the building I stumble at the threshold. I meet with a national government instead of a federal union of sovereign states." How can such a government, he asked, legislate for the "free internal government of one people living in climates so remote and whose 'habits and particular interests' are and probably always will be so different?"

Most of the Anti-Federalist leaders agreed that the central government must have more power, but they also insisted that the Convention had gone too far in limiting the power of the states. However, they were willing to accept the Constitution if certain political features were removed. They did not object to economic restraints upon the states, for a Richard Henry Lee was as opposed to paper money as a Gouverneur Morris. The Anti-Federalists quibbled about many political details, as had the members of the Convention, but in essence they objected to the very nature of the new Constitution itself. It provided, if not at once, then in the future, for a "national" and not a "federal" government.

The labels used at the time have misled posterity, but they did not mislead the principal debaters on both sides of the ratification controversy, whatever effect the labels may have had on the voters. As a Frenchman pointed out in 1794 in an effort to explain American party differences to his government, "from a whimsical contradiction the name and the real opinion of the parties" were different. The Federalists, he said, "aimed and still aim, with all their power, to annihilate federalism," while the Anti-Federalists "have always wished to preserve it. This contrast was created by the Consolidators or the Constitutionalists, who, being the first in giving the denominations (a matter so important in a revolution) took for themselves that which was the most popular, though in reality it contradicted their ideas. . . ."

Because the distinction was understood by the leaders, a significant portion of the debate centered around this issue. The men who now called themselves Federalists, but who had argued for a national government in the Convention, declared that the new Constitution provided for a federal government of strictly limited and sharply defined powers. Their opponents disagreed, and even anonymous newspaper writers cited the plain dictionary meaning of the words "federal" and "national."

The debate began as soon as the Constitution was published, and within three weeks James Wilson made a public speech in Philadelphia defending it and outlining the arguments that most of the self-styled Federalists were to use in the press and in the ratifying conventions in the months to come. He denied that the Constitution provided for a "consolidated" or national government which would swallow up the states. Congress, he said, had only delegated authority, and all power "which is not given is reserved." There was no design to annihilate the states; the "federal" government in fact was dependent upon the states for its existence. Wilson cited as evidence the method of electing representatives, senators, and the president.

Wilson elaborated such arguments during the Pennsylvania ratifying convention. In the Constitutional Convention he had been a bitter opponent of equal representation of the states in the senate, but in the Pennsylvania convention he declared such equality proved that one "favorite object" of the Convention had been to "preserve the state governments unimpaired. . . ." And he repeated over and over again the argument that the central government could not exist without the state governments because of the methods of elections.

His opponents challenged him at every point. He used the preamble of the Constitution to prove that the people, not the states or the central government, were sovereign, and that the people retained all powers not expressly delegated. Robert Whitehill argued that the preamble demonstrated something quite different: " 'We the people of the United States' is a sentence that evidently shows the old foundation of the union is destroyed, the principle of confederation excluded, and a new and unwieldy system of consolidated empire is set up upon the ruins of the present compact between the states." Where Wilson talked of strictly delegated powers, Whitehill pointed out that in addition to the enumerated powers, "we find in this constitution an authority is given to make all laws that are necessary to carry it effectually into operation, and what laws are necessary is a consideration left for Congress to decide." This single line, he said, is "sufficient matter for weeks of debate. . . ."

John Smilie supported Whitehill by arguing that the particular details of the Constitution so often cited by Wilson were not the portions that threatened the states. The threat would come from "the silent but certain operation of the powers, and not the cautious, but artful tenor of the expressions contained in this system. . . . The flattery of language was, indeed, necessary to disguise the baneful purpose, but it is like the dazzling polish bestowed upon an instrument of death; and the visionary prospect of a magnificent, yet popular government was the most specious mode of rendering the people accessory to the ruin of those systems which they have so recently and so ardently labored to establish." He then spelled out specifically what he meant: the preamble was proof of a consolidated government; the taxing power of Congress was absolute; the "general welfare" clause gave unlimited power; the control of military forces left the states helpless to defend themselves; and the oath to support the Constitution required of all state officers would act upon the consciences as well as the persons of men. All this proved to him that the result, in the end, would be the establishment of a "consolidated government" and the annihilation of the states.

Such arguments in Pennsylvania and elsewhere finally forced some of the Federalists to concede that the Constitution provided for a government at least partly national in character. Thus Madison in *The Federalist* No. 39 took a middle position between extremists on either side, and in a very real sense he was right. The extreme "nationalists" in the Convention had been forced to yield to the "federalists" and the middle-of-the-roaders. The Constitution thus contains both federal and national features, a fact which has led to confusion and endless controversy ever since 1787. But at the same time this dual character has made possible a flexibility of interpretation that is a source of strength. By comparison the Articles of Confederation was an extremely rigid constitution. It was so carefully written that it was impossible to add power to the central government by "interpretation," and it was almost impossible to amend.

Because the Constitution contains general statements giving Congress the power to pass laws "necessary and proper" and for the "general welfare," and the "supremacy of the laws" clause which has allowed the national courts to review state legislative and judicial proceedings, it has been possible for the central government to transcend the apparent constitutional limitations on its power. The Constitution has been and continues to be changed by judicial interpretation of the powers of the central government, and by Congress's definition and redefinition of the meaning of "necessary and proper" and the "general welfare." Thus a constitution written for one age, and virtually unchanged by amendment, has been adjusted to a world which the Founding Fathers could not have conceived of in their wildest dreams.

The Central Government and the State of the Economy. For the past half century American historians have heatedly debated *An Economic Interpretation of the Constitution of the United States*. The idea of a direct relationship between economic interests and the writing of the Constitution has been accepted by some and violently denied by others. Above all, the assertion that the Founding Fathers of 1787 had a direct interest in the outcome of their labors, that many of them were holders of revolutionary war bonds which the new government paid off at face value, was shocking to many and treated as an attack on the very foundations of the Constitution itself. Charles A. Beard was denounced when the book appeared in 1913 and is still attacked vehemently.

This controversy would have bewildered eighteenth-century leaders on both sides of the debate over ratification. Those men took for granted the existence of a direct relationship between the economic life of a state or a nation and its government and believed that there always had been and always would be such a relationship. They differed, however, as to economic conditions at the time and the responsibility, or lack thereof, of the state and central governments for those conditions. They differed, too, as to what sections or groups within the nation should be protected and encouraged by government action. They were convinced that by legislation they could shape the economic future of the nation, but they disagreed profoundly over what that future should be. Should the government encourage agriculture, or commerce, or industry, or some combination of these three major areas of economic life?

Furthermore, eighteenth-century leaders would not have been shocked by the idea that the public creditors had a direct interest in government policy. Their political influence was a matter of common knowledge and had been discussed in the newspapers and in private letters ever since 1781. Nor were those leaders as naïve as some twentieth-century historians who assume it mattered whether or not public creditors were members of the Convention or of the state ratifying conventions—they understood that political influence was not limited by mere membership in a political body. Public creditors were a powerful force, as the members of the Convention realized, and they assumed that the creditors would support the new government. So did the newspapers. For example, during the Convention several printed an item declaring that

> One of the first objects with the national government to be elected under the new Constitution . . . will be to provide funds for the payment of the national debt. . . . Every holder of a public security of any kind is, therefore,

deeply interested in the cordial reception and speedy establishment of a vigorous continental government.

The only disagreement, and it was a major one both during the Convention and after the establishment of the new government, was over how much the public creditors should be paid. Many a journalistic tear was shed for the "widows and orphans" whose husbands and fathers had died in the war and who were starving because their holdings in the public debt were unpaid. But knowledgeable men were aware that most of the national debt had been bought up by a relatively few speculators at far less than its face value.

The opponents of the Constitution did not argue that the debt should not be paid, but they did lump public creditors together with other groups as the most strenuous advocates of adoption. Thus, one New York writer declared that among the "violent partisans" for having the people "gulp down the gilded pill blindfolded" were the society of Cincinnati, "holders of public securities, men of great wealth and expectations of public office, bankers and lawyers; these with their train of dependents from the aristocratic combination," and above all, the lawyers, keep up an incessant declamation for adoption: "like greedy gudgeons they long to satiate their stomachs with the golden bait. . . ."

Nevertheless, concern with the public creditors was only a part of the economic debate during the ratification controversy. The Federalists insisted that the country was on the verge of economic chaos which could be averted only by a speedy adoption of the Constitution. During the Convention at least two newspapers printed an article asserting that all private and public enterprise was at a standstill, awaiting the outcome of "our national Convention." States were neglecting roads and bridges; merchants had suspended voyages and manufacturers had stopped producing; money lenders had locked up their funds until they would be protected from paper money and tender laws; wealthy farmers refused to buy lands; poor farmers and tenants had stopped migrating to the frontier until given national protection from the Indians, and protection by a national system of taxation "from the more terrible hosts of state and county tax-gatherers"; public creditors, fearing the loss of their certificates, were now placing all their hopes of justice "in an enlightened and stable national government."

During the next few months, the picture of economic chaos continued to be a basic part of the argument for speedy ratification. Thus, in October a Boston newspaper described the unequal taxes, bankruptcies, jobless mechanics, and ships rotting in harbors and excluded from nearly all the ports of the world. A few weeks later the same paper declared that if the Constitution were ratified, trade would revive, farm produce spoiling in farmers' hands would be sold, all kinds of new businesses would be established, wealthy men would loan their surplus riches at low interest to encourage the arts, manufactures, and commerce, and finally, that Boston would emerge from depression and resume its former place.

The opponents of the Constitution were challenged to refute this picture of the economic difficulties of the time and they tried to. They admitted that problems existed, but insisted that they were partly the result of a long and exhausting war and partly the result of extravagant importations of foreign goods after the war. They pointed out, as did one New York writer, that a new government would not relieve merchants from debts owed to foreign merchants as a result of both pre-war and post-war importations. Such private debts were the major source of trouble, and no government could solve the problem. Still other writers pointed to the abundance of food, to the rapid expansion of trade and population, as evidence that the newspaper tales of economic stagnation were without foundation. And over and over again, the opponents of ratification insisted that tales of chaos and potential anarchy were always used by would-be tyrants to achieve power. As one writer put it: "I deny that we are in immediate danger of anarchy and commotions. Nothing but the passions of wicked and ambitious men will put us in the least danger on this head. Those who are anxious to precipitate a measure will always tell us that the present is the critical moment, now is the time, the crisis is arrived, and the present minute must be seized. Tyrants have always made use of the plea; but nothing in our circumstances can justify it." He then pointed to the profound peace of the country, the beginnings of industry and frugality after the post-war spending spree, and the sales of western lands. In other words, he argued, there was time to discuss the Constitution calmly and propose amendments and alterations. There would be no tumults unless brought about by "those artful and ambitious men who are determined to cram this government down the throats of the people before they have time deliberately to examine it."

So far as actual economic conditions are concerned, even this brief review will indicate that the debate had most of the characteristics of any modern political campaign. Then as now those who wanted political power viewed with alarm; those who wanted to stay in power admitted difficulties, but viewed matters in a much brighter light. In such campaigns the actual condition of the economy is often irrelevant so far as the campaigners are concerned.

The propaganda for and against ratification of the Constitution has made it difficult to arrive at any definitive picture of the economy of the times, but the final word on the subject might well be that of George Washington, who wrote to LaFayette in 1788 that only one more state was needed to ratify the Constitution,

> and then, I expect that many blessings will be attributed to our new government, which are now taking their rise from that industry and frugality into the practice of which the people have been forced from necessity. I really believe that there never was so much labor and economy to be found before in the country as at the present moment. If they persist in the habits they are acquiring, the good effects will soon be distinguishable. When the people shall find themselves secure under an energetic government, when foreign nations shall be disposed to give us equal advantages in commerce from dread of retaliation, when the burdens of war shall be in a manner done away by the sale of western lands, when the seeds of happiness which are sown here shall begin to expand themselves, and when everyone (under his own vine and fig-tree) shall begin to taste the fruits of freedom, then all these blessings (for all these blessings will come) will be referred to the fostering influence of the new government. Whereas many causes will have conspired to produce them.

The Debate Over a Bill of Rights. The Convention's refusal to attach a bill of rights to the Constitution was a major obstacle to ratification. The bills of rights in the first state constitutions had summed up the political ideals of the Revolution and reflected the attitudes and feelings of many of the people, and of such leaders as Samuel Adams, Richard Henry Lee, and George Mason. Appeals to those ideals had been an integral part of the pre-war argument against British encroachments on American rights, and since 1776 had been used to justify demands for social and political change. In 1787-1788 the opponents of the Constitution cited the omission of a bill of rights as proof of the sinister motives of its creators. Some were concerned above all with protecting the rights of individuals against the power of government; others were alarmed at the fundamental revolution in government explicit and implicit in the new Constitution.

At the end of the Convention, George Mason summed up more succinctly than most the argument of those who insisted upon a bill of rights as a condition of ratification. On his copy of the draft constitution of September 12, he wrote: "There is no Declaration of Rights, and the laws of the general government being paramount to the laws and constitution[s] of the several states, the Declaration of Rights in the separate states are no security." Mason thus expressed his principal objection to the Constitution, while others such as Patrick Henry and George Clinton probably objected more to the transfer of sovereignty from the states to the central government. But whatever the motives of the leaders, the lack of a bill of rights was a major issue in several states, and the decisive issue in such key states as Massachusetts and Virginia, which would not have ratified if the Federalists had not promised that a bill of rights would be added to the Constitution once the new government was in operation.

The serious debate began in Pennsylvania, where, as elsewhere, the argument over a bill of rights was but a part of the broad controversy concerning the nature of the Constitution. Did it provide for a "national" or a "federal" government? James Wilson insisted in his speech of October 6 that since the new government would be one of strictly delegated powers, it would not be a "national" or "consolidated" government. Therefore, a bill of rights was unnecessary, and to have included one in a Constitution which did not divest the people of any of their rights would have been superfluous and absurd. The government would have no power over the press, jury trial was not abolished, there was no danger from a standing army, and the supreme court was no threat because it was regulated by Congress "which is a faithful representative of the people. . . ." Later, in the Pennsylvania ratifying convention, Wilson asserted that the preamble contained the "essence of all the bills of rights that have been or can be devised, for it establishes at once that in the great article of government, the people have a right to do what they please." He said, too, that the Convention would have spurned the inclusion of a statement that any power not delegated was reserved as "an insult to the common understanding of mankind." And more than once he insisted that the enumeration of the rights of the people would be dangerous because it would be assumed that any omitted from the list had been surrendered.

Wilson did not convince his opponents in Pennsylvania any more than similar arguments convinced the opposition in other states. Four days after his speech in the State House Yard, a newspaper writer called it "extremely futile." If all powers not given were reserved, why did not the Constitution include the second article of the Confederation? The laws of Congress would be paramount to state laws; furthermore, Congress could interpret the powers given to it, and use a standing army to tyrannize over the people. The judicial power of the United States was so great that the liberty of the press could be destroyed. The writer concluded that "wherever the powers of a government extend to the lives, the persons, and properties of the subject, all of their rights ought to be clearly and expressly defined; otherwise they have but a poor security for their liberties. . . ."

John Smilie and Robert Whitehill answered Wilson in the Pennsylvania ratifying convention. Smilie declared that the preamble meant something far different from documents such as the Pennsylvania bill of rights and the Declaration of Independence. And if, as Wilson had argued, an enumeration of rights would be dangerous, why did the Constitution declare that the writ of habeas corpus and jury trial in criminal cases should not be suspended or infringed? How did the inclusion of such rights in the Constitution agree "with the maxim that whatever is not given is reserved?" Smilie thus turned Wilson's argument against him and insisted that an explicit bill of rights was needed. "So loosely, so inaccurately are the powers which are enumerated in this Constitution defined, that it will be impossible, without a test of that kind, to ascertain the limits of authority, and to declare when government has degenerated into oppression."

After appealing to the revolutionary conviction that "it is the nature of power to seek its own augmentation," Robert Whitehill declared that the preamble proved that the purpose of the Constitution was to destroy "the old foundation of the union" and set up "a new and unwieldy system of consolidated empire" on the ruins of "the present compact between the states." Hence a bill of rights was all the more necessary, although Whitehill preferred the outright rejection of a plan designed to abolish the independence and sovereignty of the states.

Wilson had no answer for such arguments except his original ones, and to the last he asserted that the Constitution was "purely democratical" in principle, although it contained the advantages of the other forms of government—that is, the monarchical and aristocratic.

The minority was convinced, as Smiley said, that "every door is shut against democracy," and at the end of the convention it proposed a bill of rights. Among other things, the bill called for a guarantee of freedom of religion, of speech, and of the press; of jury trials in both state and national courts; and of freedom from unwarranted search and seizure. It proposed various structural changes in the Constitution and concluded with a final amendment guaranteeing the sovereignty of the states and restricting the powers of the United States to those specifically delegated—that is, the second article of the Confederation. The triumphant majority rejected the amendments and refused to allow them to be entered on the journals of the convention.

When the Massachusetts convention met on January 9, 1788, the situation was the reverse of Pennsylvania's: the majority opposed ratification. The demand for a bill of rights had been an issue in that state from the beginning, with the Federalists insisting that a bill was unnecessary. A month before the convention met, the *Massachusetts Centinel* offered the standard argument: a bill of rights might be needed in "a government merely national" where there would be no check between the governing power and the people, but since the Constitution provided for "a federal government in every point of view," there was no need for one.

In the convention the Federalists repeated many of the arguments James Wilson had used in Pennsylvania: the government was not a "consolidated" one, the whole Constitution was a bill of rights, it would be dangerous to enumerate the rights of the people since some might be omitted. The opponents were not impressed, and believed, one of them said, that "notwithstanding the Wilsonian oratory," a bill of rights was needed. Why, asked another, if all powers not delegated are retained, does not the Constitution contain a bill of rights making it plain that such is the case? The Federalists admitted privately that such arguments were compelling. Rufus King wrote Washington that "an apprehension that the liberties of the people are in danger and a distrust of men of property or education have a more powerful effect on the minds of our opponents than any specific objections against the Constitution."

The Federalists who at first argued against a bill of rights were at last forced to agree to one lest ratification be defeated. They drafted some amendments, the principal one of which declared that "all powers not expressly delegated to Congress are reserved to the several states, to be by them exercised." The amendments were handed to Governor John Hancock, the president of the convention, who had not attended because of an attack of the gout—an attack which his enemies attributed to political rather than physical origins. He now appeared (lured also by the hint that he would be president if Virginia did not ratify) and presented the amendments. Samuel Adams, who had opposed the Constitution, now declared that the reservation of all powers not delegated was a summary of a bill of rights. However, he raised a question which was to be a central one in the Virginia and New York conventions: should not ratification be conditional upon the addition of such amendments to the Constitution? He was afraid that the difficult amending process would prevent adoption of amendments if the Constitution were ratified without them. He thus anticipated the arguments of Patrick Henry, and he also, perhaps, doubted the sincerity of the Massachusetts Federalists. Certainly General Thompson did, for he pointed out that those who had originally argued that the Constitution was perfect and needed no amendments were now saying that it was imperfect and needed them. He refused to say "amen" to the amendments, "but they might be voted for by some men—he did not say Judases." His suspicion was confirmed shortly after Massachusetts ratified when the Federalists began a bitter newspaper campaign against anyone who continued to demand amendments.

The Virginia convention did not meet until June 2, 1788, and its members seemed equally divided. By that time eight states had ratified and it seemed likely that New Hampshire would soon do so, thus providing the nine states required to begin a new government under the Constitution. This did not prevent the Virginians from carrying on the greatest of all the debates over ratification. The Virginia leaders, unlike those of most states, were split down the middle. In December 1787 Madison wrote to Jefferson: "It is worthy of remark that whilst in Virginia and some other states in the middle and southern districts of the union the men of intelligence, patriotism, property, and independent circumstances are thus divided, all of this description, with a few exceptions, in the eastern states and most of the middle states are zealously attached to the proposed constitution." And during the convention Washington commented: "It is a little strange that the men of large property in the South should be more afraid that the Constitution will produce an aristocracy or a monarchy than the genuine democratical people of the East."

Washington, Madison, and other powerful leaders supported ratification; equally potent leaders including Patrick Henry, Richard Henry Lee, George Mason, and Benjamin Harrison opposed it. The campaign began long before the convention met, and much of it turned around the issue of amendments. By December 1787 Madison was reporting (with remarkable accuracy as it turned out) that Virginia was divided into three parties. The first, with Washington at the head, was for adoption without amendments. The second, headed by Mason and Edmund Randolph, was for adopting with amendments which did not affect the "substance of the government," but which provided additional safeguards for the states and for the people. The third party, led by Patrick Henry, agreed with those who wanted amendments, but would probably "contend for such as strike at the essence of the system, and must lead to an adherence to the principle of the existing Confederation. . . ."

When the Virginia convention met, Patrick Henry attacked the Constitution with all his incomparable eloquence. The purpose was to create a "consolidated government," and the use of the term "We the people" in the preamble proved it. He denounced the failure to attach a bill of rights and asserted that the complex amending process was the very negation of the idea of democracy. George Mason supported Henry because the Confederation was to be replaced by a "national government" and because he doubted that a "consolidated government can preserve the freedom and secure the rights of the people." However, he would vote for the Constitution if amendments which would "secure the great essential rights of the people shall be agreed to. . . ."

James Madison was the principal defender of the Constitution and the most persistent opponent of a bill of rights. He argued, as he had in Philadelphia, that the great danger in republics was that the majority would trample on the rights of the minority, not that the people would lose their rights. This, he said, was true of all republics both ancient and modern, and would be true of the United States in the future.

He argued too (as he had earlier in *Federalist* No. 39) that the government was not purely national, but a mixture of federal and national features. As for Henry's argument that the preamble proved an intention to create a "national government," Madison declared: "Who are the parties to it? The people—but not the people as composing one great body; but the people as composing thirteen sovereignties." No state could be bound by the Constitution except by its own consent. Thus he committed himself, whether he knew it or not, against the interpretation to be placed upon the Constitution by men such as Wilson and Hamilton in the years ahead.

Such arguments did not convince the opposition which early in the convention began demanding amendments—and above all a bill of rights. Furthermore, it insisted that the Constitution be amended before Virginia ratified. The Federalists bitterly opposed such a conditional ratification, but as in Massachusetts they were at last forced to make concessions. George Wythe offered a form of ratification which attempted to answer some of the most powerful objections to the Constitution. He admitted "its imperfection," but said that Virginia should ratify and suggest any needed amendments to the first Congress. He proposed a form of ratification declaring that the powers granted by the people could be resumed whenever they were perverted, that every power not granted was retained by the people, that no right of any kind could be tampered with by the United States, and that among the "essential rights" to be so protected were freedom of conscience and the press.

Patrick Henry scorned the compromise. The proposed form itself was an admission of the Constitution's great defects, and the inference was that if some rights were enumerated, others would be surrendered. The idea of subsequent amendments was ridiculous. Henry then presented a bill of rights containing 20 articles and 20 structural amendments. He said these should be sent to the other states for consideration before Virginia ratified. He was supported by Mason, Dawson, Grayson, and others.

Madison attacked all of the amendments and prophesied confusion if Henry's advice were followed. Again he argued that the central government would be one of strictly delegated powers and that amendments were therefore unnecessary. And like James Wilson and others he argued that an enumeration of rights would be dangerous, for if any were omitted they would be presumed to be surrendered. But even Madison had to yield in the end. He agreed that some of Henry's amendments might be added after ratification, "not because they are necessary, but because they can produce no possible danger, and may gratify some gentlemen's wishes." But he would not consent to a conditional ratification with "previous amendments because they are pregnant with dreadful dangers." Henry replied in a long speech which was ended only by the competition of a great thunderstorm.

The Federalists then called for a vote the next day. At that point they were challenged by men who had not been heard from before—men who wanted to know what

amendments would be proposed to the new Congress before they would vote one way or another. Madison again
talked about the danger of a bill of rights, but once more
he promised not to oppose harmless amendments, and
insisted that it would be easy to obtain them after the new
government was in operation. Henry and his followers
continued to demand prior amendments—that is, conditional ratification—but they lost. However, they won a
major victory by forcing the convention to adopt Henry's
bill of rights and his 20 structural amendments as the
price of ratification. (*See Reading No. 5.*) The first of the
latter declared that "each state in the union shall respectively retain every power, jurisdiction, and right which is
not by this Constitution delegated to the Congress of the
United States or to the departments of the federal government." The Federalists also had to agree to instruct the
Virginia delegates in the first Congress to do all in their
power to win adoption of the bill of rights and the amendments and to conform to the spirit of the amendments in
voting on legislation.

The price was high, from the Federalist point of view,
but they had to pay it to win ratification by the narrow
margin of 10 votes (89-79). And Madison paid the price
of the undying enmity of Patrick Henry, who nearly succeeded in exiling him to the political wilderness forever.

— 14 —

THE PROCESS OF RATIFICATION

The Constitution was ratified with astonishing rapidity
compared to the time spent in futile efforts to amend the
Articles of Confederation. Delaware ratified first, on
December 7, 1787, and New Hampshire, the ninth state
needed to launch the new government, on June 21, 1788,
followed by Virginia on June 25 and New York on July

26. Only Rhode Island and North Carolina refused to ratify at the time.

The Federalist leaders believed that the best chance of ratification lay in speed, and they proceeded with dispatch and efficiency. They had several advantages. They were men who had spent years campaigning for a stronger central government, and most of them were located in seacoast cities or close to the tidewater, as in Virginia and North Carolina. Many of them had been members of the Philadelphia Convention, where they had hammered out most of the arguments they were to use in the ratification controversy. There is in fact a remarkable similarity of arguments used for adoption in the state conventions all the way from South Carolina to New Hampshire. Thus, the Federalists were able to meet arguments against the Constitution with a solidarity that their opponents seldom matched, at least on the level of the particular details of the Constitution.

In addition, most newspapers favored ratification, and where they did not, pressure was brought to bear on publishers, as in New York, Philadelphia, and Boston, to exclude a good deal of the Anti-Federalist writing. There were charges, too, that postmasters tampered with or delayed the letters of Anti-Federalist leaders, and the time that it took for letters to go between some of them lent color to the charge.

The Anti-Federalist leaders labored under great disadvantages. Most of them were either publicly or privately committed to the proposition that the central government needed more power, and hence they were in at least a superficially untenable position in opposing a Constitution which provided for such power. Their insistence that the Convention had gone "too far" was a weak argument at best, at least in popular appeal. Hence, the Anti-Federalists were forced into the position of predicting what would happen in the future on the basis of the intangibles of the Constitution. The fact that many of their predictions turned out to be right was of no immediate value in combating the Federalist argument, however false, that the new Constitution provided for no fundamental changes except in a few limited and specific areas, and that nothing could be implied except what was spelled out in definite terms in the document. Then too, many Anti-Federalist leaders, like most political leaders of the eighteenth century, came from the upper group in society. Therefore they were in sympathy with many of the basic aims of the Federalists, such as the abolition of paper money and the protection of property from state legislative attacks. In a sense, therefore, many Anti-Federalists elected to the state conventions did not represent the convictions of the men who voted for them, and enough of them shifted their votes to make ratification possible in some states.

Far more research is needed before we can know, if ever, how many men actually voted for delegates to the state conventions. An old guess that about 160,000 voted —that is, not more than a fourth or fifth of the total adult male population—is probably as good as any. About 100,000 of these men voted for supporters of the Constitution and about 60,000 for its opponents. But some men at the time asserted that the conventions did not represent popular opinion. Aedanus Burke in South Carolina claimed that four-fifths of the people in that state were opposed. Men agreed that at least a majority of the people in New Hampshire, Massachusetts, and New York were opposed, and even greater numbers in Rhode Island and North Carolina.

More important than such guesses was the regional distribution of the vote within states. The most recent study provides convincing evidence that the essential split was between the cities and the nearby commercial farming areas in support of the Constitution, and the farming backcountry in opposition. American merchants, wherever they were, supported ratification overwhelmingly, and they won the support of the artisans and mechanics of their towns and of the farmers who had direct economic ties with the towns. Aedanus Burke declared that in South Carolina the Constitution was supported by "all the rich leading men along the seacoast, and rice settlements, with few exceptions; lawyers, physicians, and divines; the merchants, mechanics, the populace and mob of Charleston." What he said of South Carolina (and always with exceptions, as he noted) could be said of a majority of the states. One New Yorker put it far more succinctly when he declared that the contest in that state was "between navigating and non-navigating individuals." There were, of course, variations from state to state in terms of broad divisions and the issues emphasized.

Ratification by the States.   Delaware ratified unanimously by a vote of 30-0 on December 7. Virtually nothing is known of what happened in that state, and it can only be assumed that Delaware citizens looked upon the Constitution as did the people around Philadelphia with whom they had such close political and economic ties. Pennsylvania ratification followed five days later, on December 12, by a vote of 46-23. The Pennsylvania Federalists had acted in haste. The legislature called a convention on September 28, the same day that Congress submitted the Constitution to the states, and the Federalist majority went so far as to stir up a mob to drag enough opponents of the Constitution into the legislature to provide a quorum. By and large the Pennsylvanians divided along the same lines that had prevailed ever since 1776. The leading supporters of the state constitution of 1776 (the "Constitutionalists") were Anti-Federalists; the opponents of that constitution (the "Republicans"), centered in Philadelphia and in other towns as far west as Pittsburgh, were the nucleus of the new Federalist party. The Constitutionalists appealed to the small farmers, whereas the Republicans were the party of the merchants, supported by the artisans and mechanics of Philadelphia and other towns on the issue of the Constitution. The eastern farming counties of Pennsylvania voted overwhelmingly for the Constitution; the backcountry farming counties almost as solidly against it.

Six days after Pennsylvania, New Jersey ratified by a vote of 39-0. In that state such political unanimity was virtually unprecedented, but its citizens now gladly accepted the new Constitution. The reason was economic. New Jersey had almost no foreign trade from which to collect revenue. It had a heavy debt which could be paid only through taxes on land, and so its citizens were anxious to unload the state debt upon the central government.

Georgia ratified unanimously (26-0) on January 2, 1788. Georgia, like New Jersey, had a serious problem. Washington put it bluntly when he said that "if a weak state with the Indians on its back and the Spaniards on its flank does not see the necessity of a general government, there must I think be wickedness or insanity in the way." The Spanish were back in Florida and the Creek Indians had no love for Georgians, and the Georgians knew it. Within a few years they were to denounce the new government, but for the moment the hope of national military protection was the overriding motive for ratification.

Connecticut was the first New England state to ratify, and it did so January 9, by a vote of 128-40. Federalists like Jeremiah Wadsworth wished that Shays's Rebellion could have lasted longer, but he need not have worried. The newspapers, the clergy, and almost every important merchant, lawyer, and officeholder supported the Constitution. Opposition came only from small farming areas, and the small farmers were no match for the men who dominated the state politically and economically.

Massachusetts was the first of the large states after Pennsylvania to meet, and it was generally agreed that if Massachusetts, or Virginia, or New York did not ratify, the new government would probably fail. In Massachusetts, more than elsewhere, the battle was looked upon as one between the rich and the poor, and it was so described by men on both sides: in the newspapers, in private letters, and in the convention debates. The Anti-Federalists are followers of Daniel Shays, asserted the *Massachusetts Centinel*. They want to abolish all government. They are a "meer junto—a few placemen, a few trimmers, and the rest men deeply in debt, who despair of paper money and tender laws, should the new system be adopted." General Knox and many another Federalist agreed. Conversely, Knox described the Federalists as "the commercial part of the state, to whom are added all the men of considerable property, the clergy, the lawyers, including all the judges of all the courts, and all the officers of the late army, and the neighborhood of all the great towns. . . ." Numerically, he estimated that the supporters of the Constitution made up about two-sevenths of the population of the state.

In Massachusetts, more than any other state, the Federalists talked about the economic benefits to be derived from the Constitution. Its merchants had long wanted "national" regulation of trade, by which they meant legislation which would help them get control of the carrying trade of the southern states. In the Convention, Dawes spoke at length on the advantages of the commercial power given to Congress. He estimated that British merchants made $300,000 in freight and other charges out of each million dollars' worth of goods shipped to London from the South. "This," said he, "is money which belongs to the New England states. . . ." And William Phillips of Boston cried eloquently that in the commercial power "the New England states have a treasure offered to them better than the mines of Peru. . . ."

In the light of such speeches, it is little wonder that the Massachusetts opponents of ratification declared that the Constitution would mean the exploitation of the poor for the benefit of the rich. Who will pay the debts of the yeomanry, asked William Wedgery of Maine? Amos Singletary of Worcester County charged that "these lawyers, and men of learning, and moneyed men, that talk so finely and gloss over matters so smoothly, to make us poor, illiterate people swallow down the pill, expect to get into Congress themselves; they expect to be the managers of this Constitution, and get all the power and all the money into their own hands, and then they will swallow up all us little folks, like the great Leviathan, Mr. President; yes, just as the whale swallowed up Jonah."

The Federalists feared such opposition, but in the end they won, as we have seen, by winning over Governor Hancock and Samuel Adams with the promise of amendments, and on February 16 the convention ratified by the slim margin of 187-168.

The New Hampshire convention met three days before Massachusetts ratified, but the votes stood 70-30 against ratification, many of the majority having specific instructions from their constituents to vote "no." The Federalists managed to bring about an adjournment until June to give some delegates a chance to seek a change in their instructions. New Hampshire's refusal to ratify sent a shock through the other states. In March, Rhode Island threw another and even greater obstacle in the way. The legislature had refused to send delegates to the Philadelphia Convention. Then in March 1788, it polled the towns and they turned down a ratifying convention, 28-2. The count in New England now stood two to two.

Maryland was the next state to meet. Ratification was opposed by some of the great leaders of the state: Samuel Chase and William Paca, signers of the Declaration, and former governor Thomas Johnson. Luther Martin and John Francis Mercer had attended the Philadelphia Convention, but had refused to stay and sign the Constitution, and Martin in particular was one of the most vigorous speakers against ratification. An alarmed Washington used all his prestige to swing Maryland leaders over, prophesying that the Constitution was doomed if Maryland did not ratify. Such fears were unfounded. Very few Anti-Federalist candidates ran for seats in the convention which met on April 21. Five days later Maryland ratified by an overwhelming 63-11 vote.

The South Carolina convention met in Charleston on May 12. The legislature had called the convention in January by the incredibly narrow margin of 76-75. This division was along the old east-west lines that had long split the state, and all but two western legislators voted against a convention. Everyone at the time agreed that the east almost solidly backed the Constitution and that the west almost solidly opposed it. Maryland's ratification disheartened the Anti-Federalist leaders, and holding the convention in Charleston where high and low alike supported ratification had its effect. Finally, eastern over-representation virtually guaranteed the result. South Carolina ratified on May 23 by a vote of 149-73.

South Carolina was the eighth state to ratify, and shortly thereafter the adjourned New Hampshire convention met once more. The Federalist leaders, in almost complete control of the press, had done their work well, and on June 21 New Hampshire ratified, 57-47. Tobias Lear, Washington's secretary, reported from Portsmouth that three-fourths of the property and a larger proportion of the abilities of the state supported the Constitution and that the opposition consisted of debtors opposed to any government that would abolish tender laws and block the issuance of paper currency. As for the amendments proposed by the convention, Lear commented that they were drawn up "with a view of softening and conciliating" the moderate opponents rather than with any expectation "that they would ever be ingrafted into the Constitution."

Nine states had now ratified, and the new government

could, in theory, be put into operation. But if it were to be effective the two great states of Virginia and New York had to ratify as well. The Virginia convention met on June 2, but the delegates were so evenly divided that neither side dared call for a vote. New York met on June 17 with Governor Clinton's Anti-Federalist forces in control, 46-19.

The Virginia debate, as we have seen, centered around the very nature of the government itself. The Federalists made some effort to picture the chaos that would follow rejection, but their efforts were subjected to biting satire and were soon abandoned. When Governor Randolph offered such an argument, William Grayson replied that doubtless "Pennsylvania and Maryland are to fall upon us from the north, like the Goths and Vandals of old; the Algerines, whose flat-sided vessels never came farther than Madeira, are to fill the Chesapeake with mighty fleets and to attack us on our front; the Indians are to invade us with numerous armies on our rear, in order to convert our cleared lands into hunting-grounds; and the Carolinians, from the south (mounted on alligators, I presume) are to come and destroy our cornfields, and eat up our little children! These sir, are the mighty dangers which await us if we reject. . . ."

Virginia ratification, as we have seen, turned on the issue of a bill of rights and of structural amendments which the Federalists had to agree to support in the first Congress. (*See Reading No. 5.*) The New York Federalists went even further to achieve ratification. Governor Clinton, as "Cato," had at once attacked the new Constitution as a national government and charged that it was "founded in usurpation" and would be dangerous to the liberty and happiness of the people. He and his agrarian party won a resounding victory in elections to the convention, where they were opposed by a minority led by the delegates from New York City and the nearby counties. Ratification by New Hampshire and Virginia was a devastating blow to the Anti-Federalists, and they were alarmed at the threat that New York City and the southern counties would secede if the convention refused to ratify. New York could not easily stay out of the union, but even so the Anti-Federalists were determined to have a bill of rights. However, they disagreed among themselves. Should ratification be conditional upon adoption of amendments, or should they put their faith in subsequent amendments? On this issue, their debates were much like those in Virginia.

New York finally ratified on July 26 by a vote of 30-27, but the Federalists had to pay an even steeper price for victory than in Virginia. The convention agreed unanimously to send a circular letter to all the state legislatures urging them to request the first Congress to call a second constitutional convention immediately to act upon the many amendments proposed by the state ratifying conventions. The New York circular letter was a shock to Madison, who was deeply afraid that a second convention would undo the work of the first. He soon decided that it would have been better if New York had not ratified on those terms and concluded that the Federalists had agreed to them to ensure the location of the national capital in New York City.

It was now possible to establish the new government. Elections were held, and in the spring of 1789 Washington was inaugurated the first President under the new Constitution. Faced with this fact, North Carolina and Rhode Island could not hold out indefinitely. The North Carolina convention met in July 1788. It adjourned in August without rejecting the Constitution outright, but it insisted that amendments must be adopted. One by one the opponents were won over, and in November 1789 a new convention ratified by a vote of 194-77. The Rhode Islanders held out the longest. The merchants of Newport and Providence kept up a steady campaign for ratification, and in the spring of 1790, the new Congress threatened to cut Rhode Island off from all intercourse with the rest of the nation. A convention met in March, adopted a list of amendments, and then adjourned until May to await the decision of the towns. The convention met again on May 24 after a state election in which the Anti-Federalists won a resounding victory. However, the convention ratified on May 29 by a vote of 34-32, and the union of the thirteen states under the Constitution was at last completed.

— 15 —

THE BILL OF RIGHTS

The final act in the making of the Constitution was the adoption of the Bill of Rights. A guarantee of the rights of individuals with which no government should or could interfere had a widespread popular appeal, and the promise to add such a guarantee to the Constitution was instrumental in securing ratification in at least three states. In addition, a good many leading opponents of the Constitution wanted to add amendments which would deprive the central government of some of its new powers, or at least spell out those powers in more precise terms.

The state conventions proposed about 150 amendments of both kinds. The Pennsylvania minority and several conventions demanded an amendment specifically declaring that all powers not "expressly" or "clearly delegated" were reserved to the states. They proposed, in other words, to write into the Constitution the second article of the Confederation, and all that it implied concerning the distribution of power between the states and the central government. Some amendments called for a variety of specific restraints upon Congress such as a two-thirds vote to pass navigation acts, borrow money, raise troops, and declare war. Others proposed to limit the power to levy direct taxes and to regulate elections within the states. Several amendments provided limitations on the jurisdiction of the national courts. However, the amendments most widely insisted upon were those guaranteeing the rights of individuals. Most of these were copied from the state bills of rights of 1776, often word for word. Each man should be guaranteed the right of freedom of speech and of religion, and the liberty of the press should be inviolate. Jury trials should be guaranteed in civil cases, and men should be free from unwarranted searches and seizures, from cruel and unusual punishments, and should not be compelled to incriminate themselves. Not only should men be guaranteed these and other rights, but Congress must be denied the power to tamper with them in any way. The bill of rights and the amendments adopted by the Virginia ratifying convention in June 1788 brought together the objections that had been raised throughout America, and were the basis of the Bill of Rights finally added to the Constitution. (*See Reading No. 5.*)

By the summer of 1788 such leaders as Patrick Henry, George Clinton, and George Mason were proposing to secure a bill of rights and limiting amendments by means of a second constitutional convention. Mason and Randolph had proposed one at Philadelphia in 1787, and the Virginia legislature had supported them. Then in July 1788 the New York convention sent a circular letter to all the state legislatures asking them to require the new Congress to call a convention, as two-thirds of the states could do under the Constitution. Virginia, North Carolina, and Rhode Island agreed, but the rest of the states ignored the circular. However, Madison grew ever more certain that the popular demand would force the other states to act as well unless the new Congress took the initiative and offered amendments on its own. Meanwhile, to win election to the house of representatives, Madison had to promise his Virginia constituents that he would work for amendments as soon as the first Congress met.

But Madison had made clear in the Virginia convention and in private letters afterwards that he did not believe in what he called "parchment barriers." Shortly before his election to Congress, he wrote to Jefferson that the great danger in governments where "the real power lies in the majority of the community" is that the majority will invade private rights, not that the government will interfere with the liberties of the people. Madison was thus once more expounding a basic conviction, but political theory had to yield to political reality.

When the first Congress met, Ralph Izard of South Carolina probably expressed the feelings of most Federalists when he said he hoped that Congress would not waste time in an idle discussion of amendments, but would "go to work immediately about the finances. . . ."

The fact was that most of the Federalists who had promised to support amendments in the state conventions had no intention of living up to their promise. But Madison insisted that Congress must adopt a bill of rights and send it along to the states. It was fortunate, he said, that so much opposition to the Constitution had been on the grounds of civil liberties. Congress could therefore remove the objection without "endangering any part of the Constitution." He warned that if Congress did not act, the public mind would be inflamed, for too many people "out of doors" were demanding amendments for Congress to ignore them. There would soon be a clamor for a second convention, and Madison declared that he was unwilling to see the door opened "for a reconsideration of the whole structure of government," and a second convention would not stop with mere amendments. Madison therefore proposed a bill of rights, based mostly on the Virginia amendments, and he included the reservation to the states of all powers not delegated to Congress —the statement that finally became the tenth amendment. He did not think it would do any harm, and the words "expressly delegated," which had been a part of the Articles of Confederation and which several state conventions had demanded, were, significantly, omitted.

The Bill of Rights was thus born of Madison's concern to prevent a second convention which might undo the work of the Philadelphia Convention, and also of his concern to save his political future in Virginia. On the other side such men as Patrick Henry understood perfectly the political motives involved. He looked upon the passage of the Bill of Rights as a political defeat which would make it impossible to block the centralization of all power in the national government. Richard Henry Lee agreed with Henry that "the most essential danger from the present system arises, in my opinion, from its tendency to a consolidated government, instead of a union of Confederated States." But Lee also clung to the convictions of 1776, as did many another American. "It must never be forgotten," he wrote, "that the liberties of the people are not so safe under the gracious manner of government, as by the limitation of power." When he saw the Bill of Rights in its final form he declared: "How wonderfully scrupulous have they been

in stating rights. The English language has been carefully culled to find words feeble in their nature or doubtful in their meaning."

The Bill of Rights was thus the product of eighteenth-
century politics, but the ideals it expressed were centuries
old then, and are ever-new today. However cynical the
motives of the politicians, enough of the American people welcomed the Bill of Rights to make it an enduring
part of the Constitution within two years of its submission
to the states. And although the Bill of Rights is sometimes
ignored or evaded, it remains an ideal for which people
may strive in the twentieth century, as they did in the
eighteenth. (*See Reading No. 6.*)

EPILOGUE

The writing and ratification of the Constitution was
but a first step in its "making," for the document provided only the bare outline of government—one that was
both federal and national in character. Men recognized
then, as they have ever since, that the government has
meaning only as it is defined by legislation, executive actions, and judicial proceedings. And since Americans
have always disagreed as to the role of the central government, congresses, presidents, judges, and the American people have been debating ever since 1789 about
the nature of the Constitution and the power of the government derived from it. Some have argued that it
should be a national government with virtually unlimited
powers and others that it should be a federal government
with restricted power over the states and the people.

Today the Constitution is outwardly the same as it was
in 1789, for it has been little changed by amendments
during one and three quarter centuries. But the actual
"constitution" extends far beyond its simple eighteenth-
century foundation. As they have sought to meet the
needs of a rapidly growing and ever more complex society, congresses, presidents, and the courts have steadily

increased the power of the central government over every aspect of the life of the nation.

Today, Americans continue to debate, as they have ever since the eighteenth century, about the division of power between the states and the central government, and about the role the latter should play in the economic and social life of the nation. Such debate had validity in an earlier and simpler age, but it is now little more than a romantic exercise. Although the Constitution itself remains what it was, the realities of political and economic life in the twentieth century have created an all-powerful national government in fact. Hence under the "constitution" as it exists in practice, the central government has almost unlimited powers. And the only limitations on the exercise of ultimate power are more dependent upon the exigencies of politics and upon the self-restraint of those who govern than upon the restraints set forth in the Constitution of 1787.

Part II

SELECTED READINGS

— Reading No. 1 —

THE VIRGINIA RESOLUTIONS, MAY 29, 1787 *

After electing George Washington presiding officer and adopting rules of procedure, the Convention got under way on May 29. Governor Edmund Randolph of Virginia made the formal opening speech and then presented the following resolutions as a basis for discussion. The resolutions had been prepared by the Virginia delegation before the opening of the Convention.

Resolutions proposed by Mr. Randolph in Convention, May 29, 1787

1. Resolved that the Articles of Confederation ought to be so corrected and enlarged as to accomplish the objects proposed by their institution; namely, "common defense, security of liberty, and general welfare."

2. Resolved therefore that the rights of suffrage in the national legislature ought to be proportioned to the quotas of contribution, or to the number of free inhabitants, as the one or the other rule may seem best in different cases.

3. Resolved that the national legislature ought to consist of two branches.

* James Madison, Notes on the Debates, in Charles C. Tansill, ed., *Documents Illustrative of the Formation of the Union of the American States* (Washington, 1927), pp. 116-119.

4. Resolved that the members of the first branch of the national legislature ought to be elected by the people of the several states every   for the term of   ; to be of the age of   years at least; to receive liberal stipends by which they may be compensated for the devotion of their time to public service; to be ineligible to any office established by a particular state, or under the authority of the United States, except those peculiarly belonging to the functions of the first branch, during the term of service, and for the space of   after its expiration; to be incapable of reelection for the space of   after the expiration of their term of service, and to be subject to recall.

5. Resolved that the members of the second branch of the national legislature ought to be elected by those of the first, out of a proper number of persons nominated by the individual legislatures, to be of the age of   years at least; to hold their offices for a term sufficient to ensure their independency; to receive liberal stipends, by which they may be compensated for the devotion of their time to public service; and to be ineligible to any office established by a particular state, or under the authority of the United States, except those peculiarly belonging to the functions of the second branch, during the term of service, and for the space of   after the expiration thereof.

6. Resolved that each branch ought to possess the right of originating acts; that the national legislature ought to be empowered to enjoy the legislative rights vested in Congress by the Confederation and moreover to legislate in all cases to which the separate states are incompetent, or in which the harmony of the United States may be interrupted by the exercise of individual legislation; to negative all laws passed by the several states, contravening in the opinion of the national legislature the articles of union; and to call forth the force of the union against any member of the union failing to fulfill its duty under the articles thereof.

7. Resolved that a national executive be instituted; to be chosen by the national legislature for the term of   years; to receive punctually at stated times a fixed compensation for the services rendered, in which no increase or diminution shall be made so as to affect the

magistracy, existing at the time of increase or diminution, and to be ineligible a second time; and that besides a general authority to execute the national laws, it ought to enjoy the executive rights vested in Congress by the Confederation.

8. Resolved that the executive and a convenient number of the national judiciary ought to compose a council of revision with authority to examine every act of the national legislature before it shall operate, and every act of a particular legislature before a negative thereon shall be final; and that the dissent of the said council shall amount to a rejection, unless the act of the national legislature be again passed or that of a particular legislature be again negatived by   of the members of each branch.

9. Resolved that a national judiciary be established to consist of one or more supreme tribunals, and of inferior tribunals, to be chosen by the national legislature, to hold their offices during good behavior; and to receive punctually at stated times fixed compensation for their services, in which no increase or diminution shall be made so as to affect the persons actually in office at the time of such increase or diminution. That the jurisdiction of the inferior tribunals shall be to hear and determine in the first instance, and of the supreme tribunal to hear and determine in the dernier resort, all piracies and felonies on the high seas, captures from an enemy; cases in which foreigners or citizens of other states applying to such jurisdictions may be interested, or which respect the collection of the national revenue; impeachments of any national officers, and questions which may involve the national peace and harmony.

10. Resolved that provision ought to be made for the admission of states lawfully arising within the limits of the United States, whether from a voluntary junction of government and territory or otherwise, with the consent of a number of voices in the national legislature less than the whole.

11. Resolved that a republican government and the territory of each state, except in the instance of a voluntary junction of government and territory, ought to be guaranteed by the United States to each state.

12. Resolved that provision ought to be made for the

continuance of Congress and their authorities and privileges, until a given day after the reform of the articles of union shall be adopted, and for the completion of all their engagements.

13. Resolved that provision ought to be made for the amendment of the articles of union whensoever it shall seem necessary, and that the assent of the national legislature ought not to be required thereto.

14. Resolved that the legislative, executive, and judiciary powers within the several states ought to be bound by oath to support the articles of union.

15. Resolved that the amendments which shall be offered to the Confederation by the convention ought, at a proper time or times after the approbation of Congress, to be submitted to an assembly or assemblies of representatives, recommended by the several legislatures to be expressly chosen by the people, to consider and decide thereon.

— Reading No. 2 —

THE PLAN FOR A NATIONAL GOVERNMENT: REPORT ON THE VIRGINIA RESOLUTIONS, JUNE 13, 19, 1787 *

Sitting as a "committee of the whole," the Convention debated the Virginia resolutions of May 29 until June 13, when it delivered a "report." It was adopted on June 19 after the rejection of the New Jersey Plan (see Reading

* James Madison, Notes on the Debates, in Charles C. Tansill, ed., *Documents Illustrative of the Formation of the Union of the American States* (Washington, 1927), pp. 201-203.

No. 3), *and was the basis of the subsequent debate which led to the writing of the first draft of the Constitution.*

✓   ✓   ✓

1. Resolved that it is the opinion of this committee that a national government ought to be established, consisting of a supreme legislative, executive, and judiciary.

2. Resolved that the national legislature ought to consist of two branches.

3. Resolved that the members of the first branch of the national legislature ought to be elected by the people of the several states for the term of three years; to receive fixed stipends by which they may be compensated for the devotion of their time to public service, to be paid out of the national treasury; to be ineligible to any office established by a particular state, or under the authority of the United States, (except those peculiarly belonging to the functions of the first branch), during the term of service, and under the national government for the space of one year after its expiration.

4. Resolved that the members of the second branch of the national legislature ought to be chosen by the individual legislatures; to be of the age of thirty years at least; to hold their offices for a term sufficient to ensure their independency, namely, seven years; to receive fixed stipends by which they may be compensated for the devotion of their time to public service, to be paid out of the national treasury; to be ineligible to any office established by a particular state, or under the authority of the United States, (except those peculiarly belonging to the functions of the second branch), during the term of service, and under the national government for the space of one year after its expiration.

5. Resolved that each branch ought to possess the right of originating acts.

6. Resolved that the national legislature ought to be empowered to enjoy the legislative rights vested in Congress by the Confederation, and moreover to legislate in all cases to which the separate states are incompetent or in which the harmony of the United States may be interrupted by the exercise of individual legislation; to negative all laws passed by the several states contravening in the opinion of the national legislature the articles

of union or any treaties subsisting under the authority of the union.

7. Resolved that the rights of suffrage in the first branch of the national legislature ought not to be according to the rule established in the Articles of Confederation, but according to some equitable ratio of representation, namely, in proportion to the whole number of white and other free citizens and inhabitants, of every age, sex, and condition, including those bound to servitude for a term of years, and three-fifths of all other persons not comprehended in the foregoing description, except Indians not paying taxes in each state.

8. Resolved that the right of suffrage in the second branch of the national legislature ought to be according to the rule established for the first.

9. Resolved that a national executive be instituted to consist of a single person, to be chosen by the national legislature for the term of seven years, with power to carry into execution the national laws; to appoint to offices in cases not otherwise provided for; to be ineligible a second time, and to be removable on impeachment and conviction of malpractices or neglect of duty; to receive a fixed stipend by which he may be compensated for the devotion of his time to public service, to be paid out of the national treasury.

10. Resolved that the national executive shall have a right to negative any legislative act, which shall not be afterwards passed unless by two-thirds of each branch of the national legislature.

11. Resolved that a national judiciary be established, to consist of one supreme tribunal, the judges of which to be appointed by the second branch of the national legislature; to hold their offices during good behavior; and to receive punctually at stated times a fixed compensation for their services, in which no increase or diminution shall be made so as to affect the persons actually in office at the time of such increase or diminution.

12. Resolved that the national legislature be empowered to appoint inferior tribunals.

13. Resolved that the jurisdiction of the national judiciary shall extend to all cases which respect the collection of the national revenue, impeachments of any na-

tional officers, and questions which involve the national peace and harmony.

14. Resolved that provision ought to be made for the admission of states lawfully arising within the limits of the United States, whether from a voluntary junction of government and territory or otherwise, with the consent of a number of voices in the national legislature less than the whole.

15. Resolved that provision ought to be made for the continuance of Congress and their authorities and privileges until a given day after the reform of the articles of union shall be adopted and for the completion of all their engagements.

16. Resolved that a republican constitution and its existing laws ought to be guaranteed to each state by the United States.

17. Resolved that provision ought to be made for the amendment of the articles of union whensoever it shall seem necessary.

18. Resolved that the legislative, executive, and judiciary powers within the several states ought to be bound by oath to support the articles of union.

19. Resolved that the amendments which shall be offered to the Confederation by the Convention ought, at a proper time or times after the approbation of Congress, to be submitted to an assembly or assemblies recommended by the several legislatures to be expressly chosen by the people to consider and decide thereon.

— Reading No. 3 —

THE PLAN FOR A STRONG FEDERAL GOVERNMENT: THE NEW JERSEY PLAN, JUNE 15, 1787 *

The report on the Virginia resolutions on June 13 (see Reading No. 2) inspired members of the Convention who wanted to strengthen the central government, but who wanted to retain both its federal structure and the equality of the states, to present a counter plan. This was placed before the Convention on June 15 by William Paterson of New Jersey.

✓   ✓   ✓

1. Resolved that the Articles of Confederation ought to be so revised, corrected, and enlarged as to render the federal constitution adequate to the exigencies of government and the preservation of the union.

2. Resolved that in addition to the powers vested in the United States in Congress by the present existing Articles of Confederation, they be authorized to pass acts for raising a revenue, by levying a duty or duties on all goods or merchandises of foreign growth or manufacture, imported into any part of the United States, by stamps on paper, vellum, or parchment, and by a postage on all letters or packages passing through the general post-office, to be applied to such federal purposes as they shall deem proper and expedient; to make rules and

* James Madison, Notes on the Debates, in Charles C. Tansill, ed., *Documents Illustrative of the Formation of the Union of the American States* (Washington, 1927), pp. 204-207.

regulations for the collection thereof, and the same from time to time, to alter and amend in such manner as they shall think proper; to pass acts for the regulation of trade and commerce as well with foreign nations as with each other, provided that all punishments, fines, forfeitures, and penalties to be incurred for contravening such acts, rules, and regulations shall be adjudged by the common law judiciaries of the states in which any offense contrary to the true intent and meaning of such acts, rules, and regulations shall have been committed or perpetrated, with liberty of commencing in the first instance all suits and prosecutions for that purpose in the superior common law judiciary in such state, subject nevertheless, for the correction of all errors, both in law and fact in rendering judgment, to an appeal to the judiciary of the United States.

3. Resolved that whenever requisitions shall be necessary, instead of the rule for making requisitions mentioned in the Articles of Confederation, the United States in Congress be authorized to make such requisitions in proportion to the whole number of white and other free citizens and inhabitants of every age, sex, and condition, including those bound to servitude for a term of years, and three-fifths of all other persons not comprehended in the foregoing description, except Indians not paying taxes; that if such requisitions be not complied with, in the time specified therein, to direct the collection thereof in the non-complying states, and for that purpose to devise and pass acts directing and authorizing the same; provided that none of the powers hereby vested in the United States in Congress shall be exercised without the consent of at least   states, and in that proportion if the number of confederated states should hereafter be increased or diminished.

4. Resolved that the United States in Congress be authorized to elect a federal executive to consist of   persons; to continue in office for the term of   years; to receive punctually at stated times a fixed compensation for their services, in which no increase or diminution shall be made so as to affect the persons composing the executive at the time of such increase or diminution, to be paid out of the federal treasury; to be incapable of holding any other office or appointment

during their time of service and for   years thereafter; to be ineligible a second time, and removable by
Congress on application by a majority of the executives
of the several states; that the executives, besides their
general authority to execute the federal acts, ought to
appoint all federal officers not otherwise provided for;
and to direct all military operations, provided that none
of the persons composing the federal executive shall on
any occasion take command of any troops, so as per-
sonally to conduct any enterprise as general or in other
capacity.

5. Resolved that a federal judiciary be established to
consist of a supreme tribunal, the judges of which to be
appointed by the executive, and to hold their offices
during good behavior; to receive punctually at stated
times a fixed compensation for their services, in which
no increase or diminution shall be made so as to affect
the persons actually in office at the time of such increase
or diminution; that the judiciary so established shall have
authority to hear and determine in the first instance on
all impeachments of federal officers, and by way of appeal in the dernier resort in all cases touching the rights
of ambassadors, in all cases of captures from an enemy,
in all cases of piracies and felonies on the high seas, in
all cases in which foreigners may be interested, in the
construction of any treaty or treaties, or which may arise
on any of the acts for regulation of trade or the collection of the federal revenue; that none of the judiciary
shall during the time they remain in office be capable of
receiving or holding any other office or appointment
during their time of service, or for thereafter.

6. Resolved that all acts of the United States in Congress made by virtue and in pursuance of the powers
hereby and by the Articles of Confederation vested in
them, and all treaties made and ratified under the authority of the United States shall be the supreme law of the
respective states so far forth as those acts or treaties shall
relate to the said states or their citizens, and that the judiciary of the several states shall be bound thereby in their
decisions, anything in the respective laws of the individual
states to the contrary notwithstanding; and that if any
state, or any body of men in any state, shall oppose or
prevent the carrying into execution such acts or treaties,

the federal executive shall be authorized to call forth the power of the confederated states, or so much thereof as may be necessary to enforce and compel an obedience to such acts or an observance of such treaties.

7. Resolved that provision be made for the admission of new states into the union.

8. Resolved the rule for naturalization ought to be the same in every state.

9. Resolved that a citizen of one state committing an offense in another state of the union shall be deemed guilty of the same offense as if it had been committed by a citizen of the state in which the offense was committed.

— Reading No. 4 —

THE CONSTITUTION OF THE UNITED STATES, SEPTEMBER 17, 1787

The following is the Constitution submitted to the Congress of the United States by the Convention. It was accompanied by a resolution stating that it was the "opinion" of the Convention that the Constitution should be ratified by state conventions, and that after nine states had ratified, Congress should set the time for elections and for the beginning of the new government.

↗   ↗   ↗

WE THE PEOPLE of the United States, in Order to form a more perfect Union, establish Justice, insure domestic Tranquility, provide for the common defence, promote the general Welfare, and secure the Blessings of Liberty to ourselves and our Posterity, do ordain and establish this Constitution for the United States of America.

ARTICLE I

SECTION 1

All legislative Powers herein granted shall be vested in a Congress of the United States, which shall consist of a Senate and House of Representatives.

SECTION 2

The House of Representatives shall be composed of Members chosen every second Year by the People of the several States, and the Electors in each State shall have the Qualifications requisite for Electors of the most numerous Branch of the State Legislature.

No person shall be a Representative who shall not have attained to the Age of twenty-five Years, and been seven Years a Citizen of the United States, and who shall not, when elected, be an Inhabitant of that State in which he shall be chosen.

Representatives and direct Taxes shall be apportioned among the several States which may be included within this Union, according to their respective Numbers, which shall be determined by adding to the whole Number of free Persons, including those bound to Service for a Term of Years, and excluding Indians not taxed, three fifths of all other Persons. The actual Enumeration shall be made within three Years after the first Meeting of the Congress of the United States, and within every subsequent Term of ten Years, in such Manner as they shall by Law direct. The Number of Representatives shall not exceed one for every thirty Thousand, but each State shall have at Least one Representative; and until such enumeration shall be made, the State of New Hampshire shall be entitled to chuse three, Massachusetts eight, Rhode-Island and Providence Plantations one, Connecticut five, New-York six, New Jersey four, Pennsylvania eight, Delaware one, Maryland six, Virginia ten, North Carolina five, South Carolina five, and Georgia three.

When vacancies happen in the Representation from any State, the Executive Authority thereof shall issue Writs of Election to fill such Vacancies.

The House of Representatives shall chuse their Speaker

and other Officers; and shall have the sole Power of Impeachment.

SECTION 3

The Senate of the United States shall be composed of two Senators from each State, chosen by the Legislature thereof, for six Years; and each Senator shall have one Vote.

Immediately after they shall be assembled in Consequence of the first Election, they shall be divided as equally as may be into three Classes. The Seats of the Senators of the first Class shall be vacated at the Expiration of the second year, of the second Class at the Expiration of the fourth Year, and of the third Class at the Expiration of the sixth Year, so that one-third may be chosen every second Year; and if Vacancies happen by Resignation, or otherwise, during the Recess of the Legislature of any State, the Executive thereof may make temporary Appointments until the next Meeting of the Legislature, which shall then fill such Vacancies.

No Person shall be a Senator who shall not have attained to the Age of thirty Years, and been nine Years a Citizen of the United States, and who shall not, when elected, be an Inhabitant of that State for which he shall be chosen.

The Vice President of the United States shall be President of the Senate, but shall have no Vote, unless they be equally divided.

The Senate shall chuse their other Officers, and also a President pro tempore, in the Absence of the Vice President, or when he shall exercise the Office of President of the United States.

The Senate shall have the sole Power to try all Impeachments. When sitting for that Purpose, they shall be on Oath or Affirmation. When the President of the United States is tried, the Chief Justice shall preside: And no Person shall be convicted without the Concurrence of two thirds of the Members present.

Judgment in Cases of Impeachment shall not extend further than to removal from Office, and disqualification to hold and enjoy any Office of honor, Trust or Profit under the United States: but the Party convicted shall nevertheless be liable and subject to Indictment, Trial, Judgment and Punishment, according to Law.

SECTION 4

The Times, Places and Manner of holding Elections for Senators and Representatives, shall be prescribed in each State by the Legislature thereof; but the Congress may at any time by Law make or alter such Regulations, except as to the Places of chusing Senators.

The Congress shall assemble at least once in every Year, and such Meeting shall be on the first Monday in December, unless they shall by Law appoint a different Day.

SECTION 5

Each House shall be the Judge of the Elections, Returns and Qualifications of its own Members, and a Majority of each shall constitute a Quorum to do Business; but a smaller Number may adjourn from day to day, and may be authorized to compel the Attendance of absent Members, in such Manner, and under such Penalties as each House may provide.

Each House may determine the Rules of its Proceedings, punish its Members for disorderly Behavior, and, with the Concurrence of two thirds, expel a Member.

Each House shall keep a Journal of its Proceedings, and from time to time publish the same, excepting such Parts as may in their Judgment require Secrecy; and the Yeas and Nays of the Members of either House on any question shall, at the Desire of one fifth of those present, be entered on the Journal.

Neither House, during the Session of Congress, shall, without the Consent of the other, adjourn for more than three days, nor to any other Place than that in which the two Houses shall be sitting.

SECTION 6

The Senators and Representatives shall receive a Compensation for their Services, to be ascertained by Law, and paid out of the Treasury of the United States. They shall in all Cases, except Treason, Felony and Breach of the Peace, be privileged from Arrest during their Attendance at the Session of their respective Houses, and in going to and returning from the same; and for any Speech or Debate in either House, they shall not be questioned in any other Place.

No Senator or Representative shall, during the Time for which he was elected, be appointed to any civil Office under the Authority of the United States, which shall have been created, or the Emoluments whereof shall have been encreased during such time; and no Person holding any Office under the United States, shall be a Member of either House during his Continuance in Office.

SECTION 7

All Bills for raising Revenue shall originate in the House of Representatives; but the Senate may propose or concur with Amendments as on other Bills.

Every Bill which shall have passed the House of Representatives and the Senate, shall, before it become a Law, be presented to the President of the United States; If he approve he shall sign it, but if not he shall return it, with his Objections to that House in which it shall have originated, who shall enter the Objections at large on their Journal, and proceed to reconsider it. If after such Reconsideration two thirds of that House shall agree to pass the Bill, it shall be sent, together with the Objections, to the other House, by which it shall likewise be reconsidered, and if approved by two thirds of that House, it shall become a Law. But in all such Cases the Votes of both Houses shall be determined by yeas and Nays, and the Names of the Persons voting for and against the Bill shall be entered on the Journal of each House respectively. If any Bill shall not be returnd by the President within ten Days (Sundays excepted) after it shall have been presented to him, the Same shall be a Law, in like Manner as if he had signed it, unless the Congress by their Adjournment prevent its Return, in which Case it shall not be a Law.

Every Order, Resolution, or Vote to which the Concurrence of the Senate and House of Representatives may be necessary (except on a question of Adjournment) shall be presented to the President of the United States; and before the Same shall take Effect, shall be approved by him, or being disapproved by him, shall be repassed by two thirds of the Senate and House of Representatives, according to the Rules and Limitations prescribed in the Case of a Bill.

SECTION 8

The Congress shall have Power To lay and collect Taxes, Duties, Imposts and Excises, to pay the Debts and provide for the common Defence and general Welfare of the United States; but all Duties, Imposts and Excises shall be uniform throughout the United States;

To borrow Money on the credit of the United States;

To regulate Commerce with foreign Nations, and among the several States, and with the Indian Tribes;

To establish an uniform Rule of Naturalization, and uniform Laws on the subject of Bankruptcies throughout the United States;

To coin Money, regulate the Value thereof, and of foreign Coin, and fix the Standard of Weights and Measures;

To provide for the Punishment of counterfeiting the Securities and current Coin of the United States;

To establish Post Offices and post Roads;

To promote the Progress of Science and useful Arts, by securing for limited Times to Authors and Inventors the exclusive Right to their respective Writings and Discoveries;

To constitute Tribunals inferior to the supreme Court;

To define and punish Piracies and Felonies committed on the high Seas, and Offences against the Law of Nations;

To declare War, grant Letters of Marque and Reprisal, and make Rules concerning Captures on Land and Water;

To raise and support Armies, but no Appropriation of Money to that Use shall be for a longer Term than two Years;

To provide and maintain a Navy;

To make Rules for the Government and Regulation of the land and naval Forces;

To provide for calling forth the Militia to execute the Laws of the Union, suppress Insurrections and repel Invasions;

To provide for organizing, arming, and disciplining, the Militia, and for governing such Part of them as may be employed in the Service of the United States, reserving to the States respectively, the Appointment of the Officers, and the Authority of training the Militia according to the discipline prescribed by Congress;

To exercise exclusive Legislation in all Cases whatsoever, over such District (not exceeding ten Miles square) as may, by Cession of particular States, and the Acceptance of Congress, become the Seat of the Government of the United States, and to exercise like Authority over all Places purchased by the Consent of the Legislature of the State in which the Same shall be, for the Erection of Forts, Magazines, Arsenals, dock-Yards, and other needful Buildings;—And

To make all Laws which shall be necessary and proper for carrying into Execution the foregoing Powers, and all other Powers vested by this Constitution in the Government of the United States, or in any Department or Officer thereof.

SECTION 9

The Migration or Importation of such Persons as any of the States now existing shall think proper to admit, shall not be prohibited by the Congress prior to the Year one thousand eight hundred and eight, but a Tax or duty may be imposed on such Importation, not exceeding ten dollars for each Person.

The Privilege of the Writ of Habeas Corpus shall not be suspended, unless when in Cases of Rebellion or Invasion the public Safety may require it.

No Bill of Attainder or ex post facto Law shall be passed.

No Capitation, or other direct, tax shall be laid, unless in Proportion to the Census or Enumeration herein before directed to be taken.

No Tax or Duty shall be laid on Articles exported from any State.

No Preference shall be given by any Regulation of Commerce or Revenue to the Ports of one State over those of another: nor shall Vessels bound to, or from, one State, be obliged to enter, clear, or pay Duties in another.

No Money shall be drawn from the Treasury, but in Consequence of Appropriations made by Law; and a regular Statement and Account of the Receipts and Expenditures of all public Money shall be published from time to time.

No Title of Nobility shall be granted by the United States: And no Person holding any Office of Profit or Trust under them, shall, without the Consent of the Congress, accept of any present, Emolument, Office, or Title, of any kind whatever, from any King, Prince, or foreign State.

SECTION 10

No State shall enter into any Treaty, Alliance, or Confederation; grant Letters of Marque and Reprisal; coin Money; emit Bills of Credit; make any Thing but gold and silver Coin a Tender in Payment of Debts; pass any Bill of Attainder, ex post facto Law, or Law impairing the Obligation of Contracts, or grant any Title of Nobility.

No State shall, without the Consent of the Congress, lay any Imposts or Duties on Imports or Exports, except what may be absolutely necessary for executing it's inspection Laws: and the net Produce of all Duties and Imposts, laid by any State on Imports or Exports, shall be for the Use of the Treasury of the United States; and all such Laws shall be subject to the Revision and Controul of the Congress.

No State shall, without the Consent of Congress, lay any Duty of Tonnage, keep Troops, or Ships of War in time of Peace, enter into any Agreement or Compact with another State, or with a foreign Power, or engage in War, unless actually invaded, or in such imminent Danger as will not admit of delay.

ARTICLE II

SECTION 1

The executive Power shall be vested in a President of the United States of America. He shall hold his Office during the Term of four Years, and, together with the Vice President, chosen for the same Term, be elected, as follows

Each State shall appoint, in such Manner as the Legislature thereof may direct, a Number of Electors, equal to the whole Number of Senators and Representatives to which the State may be entitled in the Congress: but no Senator or Representative, or Person holding an Office of Trust or Profit under the United States, shall be appointed an Elector.

The Electors shall meet in their respective States, and vote by Ballot for two Persons, of whom one at least shall not be an Inhabitant of the same State with themselves. And they shall make a List of all the Persons voted for, and of the Number of Votes for each; which List they shall sign and certify, and transmit sealed to the Seat of the Government of the United States, directed to the President of the Senate. The President of the Senate shall, in the Presence of the Senate and House of Representatives, open all the Certificates, and the Votes shall then be counted. The Person having the greatest Number of Votes shall be the President, if such Number be a Majority of the whole Number of Electors appointed; and if there be more than one who have such Majority, and have an equal Number of Votes, then the House of Representatives shall immediately chuse by Ballot one of them for President; and if no Person have a Majority, then from the five highest on the List the said House shall in like Manner chuse the President. But in chusing the President, the Votes shall be taken by States, the Representation from each State having one Vote; A quorum for this Purpose shall consist of a Member or Members from two thirds of the States, and a Majority of all the States shall be necessary to a Choice. In every Case, after the Choice of the President, the Person having the greatest Number of Votes of the Electors shall be the Vice President. But if there should remain two or more who have equal Votes, the Senate shall chuse from them by Ballot the Vice President.

The Congress may determine the Time of chusing the Electors, and the Day on which they shall give their Votes; which Day shall be the same throughout the United States.

No Person except a natural born Citizen, or a Citizen of the United States, at the time of the Adoption of this Constitution, shall be eligible to the Office of President; neither shall any Person be eligible to that Office who shall not have attained to the Age of thirty five Years, and been fourteen Years a Resident within the United States.

In Case of the Removal of the President from Office, or of his Death, Resignation, or Inability to discharge the Powers and Duties of the said Office, the same shall devolve on the Vice President, and the Congress may by Law provide for the Case of Removal, Death, Resignation or Inability, both of the President and Vice President, declaring what Officer shall then act as President, and such Officer shall act accordingly, until the Disability be removed, or a President shall be elected.

The President shall, at stated Times, receive for his Services, a Compensation, which shall neither be increased nor diminished during the Period for which he shall have been elected, and he shall not receive within that Period any other Emolument from the United States, or any of them.

Before he enter on the Execution of his Office, he shall take the following Oath or Affirmation:—"I do solemnly swear (or affirm) that I will faithfully execute the Office of President of the United States, and will to the best of my Ability, preserve, protect and defend the Constitution of the United States."

SECTION 2

The President shall be Commander in Chief of the Army and Navy of the United States, and of the Militia of the several States, when called into the actual Service of the United States; he may require the Opinion, in writing, of the principal Officer in each of the executive Departments, upon any Subject relating to the Duties of their respective Offices, and he shall have Power to grant Reprieves and Pardons for Offences against the United States, except in Cases of Impeachment.

He shall have Power, by and with the Advice and Consent of the Senate, to make Treaties, provided two thirds of the Senators present concur; and he shall nominate, and by and with the Advice and Consent of the Senate, shall appoint Ambassadors, other public Ministers and Consuls, Judges of the supreme Court, and all other Officers of the United States, whose Appointments are not herein otherwise provided for, and which shall be established by Law: but the Congress may by Law vest the Appointment of such inferior Officers, as they think proper, in the President alone, in the Courts of Law, or in the Heads of Departments.

The President shall have Power to fill up all Vacancies that may happen during the Recess of the Senate, by granting Commissions which shall expire at the End of their next Session.

SECTION 3

He shall from time to time give to the Congress Information of the State of the Union, and recommend to their Consideration such Measures as he shall judge necessary and expedient; he may, on extraordinary Occasions, convene both Houses, or either of them, and in Case of Disagreement between them, with Respect to the Time of Adjournment, he may adjourn them to such Time as he shall think proper; he shall receive Ambassadors and other public Ministers; he shall take Care that the Laws be faithfully executed, and shall Commission all the Officers of the United States.

SECTION 4

The President, Vice President and all civil Officers of the United States, shall be removed from Office on Impeachment for, and Conviction of, Treason, Bribery, or other high Crimes and Misdemeanors.

ARTICLE III

SECTION 1

The judicial Power of the United States, shall be vested in one supreme Court, and in such inferior Courts as the Congress may from time to time ordain and establish. The Judges, both of the supreme and inferior Courts, shall hold their Offices during good Behaviour, and shall, at stated Times, receive for their Services, a Compensation, which shall not be diminished during their Continuance in Office.

SECTION 2

The judicial Power shall extend to all Cases, in Law and Equity, arising under this Constitution, the Laws of the United States, and Treaties made, or which shall be made, under their Authority;—to all Cases affecting Ambassadors, other public Ministers and Consuls;—to all Cases of admiralty and maritime Jurisdiction;—to Controversies to which the United States shall be a Party;—to Controversies between two or more States;—between a State and Citizens of another State;—between Citizens of different States,—between Citizens of the same State claiming Lands under Grants of different States, and between a State, or the Citizens thereof, and foreign States, Citizens or Subjects.

In all Cases affecting Ambassadors, other public Ministers and Consuls, and those in which a State shall be Party, the supreme Court shall have original Jurisdiction. In all the other Cases before mentioned, the supreme Court shall have appellate Jurisdiction, both as to Law and Fact, with such Exceptions, and under such Regulations as the Congress shall make.

The Trial of all Crimes, except in Cases of Impeachment, shall be by Jury; and such Trial shall be held in the State where the said Crimes shall have been committed; but when not committed within any State, the Trial shall be at such Place or Places as the Congress may by Law have directed.

Section 3

Treason against the United States, shall consist only in levying War against them, or in adhering to their Enemies, giving them Aid and Comfort. No Person shall be convicted of Treason unless on the Testimony of two Witnesses to the same overt Act, or on Confession in open Court.

The Congress shall have Power to declare the Punishment of Treason, but no Attainder of Treason shall work Corruption of Blood, or Forfeiture except during the Life of the Person attainted.

ARTICLE IV

Section 1

Full Faith and Credit shall be given in each State to the public Acts, Records, and judicial Proceedings of every other State. And the Congress may by general Laws prescribe the Manner in which such Acts, Records and Proceedings shall be proved, and the Effect thereof.

SECTION 2

The Citizens of each State shall be entitled to all Privileges and Immunities of Citizens in the several States.

A Person charged in any State with Treason, Felony, or other Crime, who shall flee from Justice, and be found in another State, shall on Demand of the executive Authority of the State from which he fled, be delivered up, to be removed to the State having Jurisdiction of the Crime.

No Person held to Service or Labour in one State, under the Laws thereof, escaping into another, shall, in Consequence of any Law or Regulation therein, be discharged from such Service or Labour, but shall be delivered up on Claim of the Party to whom such Service or Labour may be due.

SECTION 3

New States may be admitted by the Congress into this Union; but no new State shall be formed or erected within the Jurisdiction of any other State; nor any State be formed by the Junction of two or more States, or Parts of States, without the Consent of the Legislatures of the States concerned as well as of the Congress.

The Congress shall have Power to dispose of and make all needful Rules and Regulations respecting the Territory or other Property belonging to the United States; and nothing in this Constitution shall be so construed as to Prejudice any Claims of the United States, or of any particular State.

SECTION 4

The United States shall guarantee to every State in this Union a Republican Form of Government, and shall protect each of them against Invasion; and on Application of the Legislature, or of the Executive (when the Legislature cannot be convened) against domestic Violence.

ARTICLE V

The Congress, whenever two thirds of both Houses shall deem it necessary, shall propose Amendments to this Constitution, or, on the Application of the Legislatures of two thirds of the several States, shall call a Convention for proposing Amendments, which, in either Case, shall be valid to all Intents and Purposes, as Part of this Constitution, when ratified by the Legislatures of three fourths of the several States, or by Conventions in three fourths thereof, as the one or the other Mode of Ratification may be proposed by the Congress; Provided that no Amendment which may be made prior to the Year One thousand eight hundred and eight shall in any Manner affect the first and fourth Clauses in the Ninth Section of the first Article; and that no State, without its Consent, shall be deprived of its equal Suffrage in the Senate.

ARTICLE VI

All Debts contracted and Engagements entered into, before the Adoption of this Constitution, shall be as valid against the United States under this Constitution, as under the Confederation.

This Constitution, and the Laws of the United States which shall be made in Pursuance thereof; and all Treaties made, or which shall be made, under the Authority of the United States, shall be the supreme Law of the Land; and the Judges in every State shall be bound thereby, any Thing in the Constitution or Laws of any State to the Contrary notwithstanding.

The Senators and Representatives before mentioned, and the Members of the several State Legislatures, and all executive and judicial Officers, both of the United States and of the several States, shall be bound by Oath or Affirmation, to support this Constitution; but no religious Test shall ever be required as a Qualification to any Office or public Trust under the United States.

ARTICLE VII

The Ratification of the Conventions of nine States, shall be sufficient for the Establishment of this Constitution between the States so ratifying the Same.

DONE in Convention by the Unanimous Consent of the States present the Seventeenth Day of September in the Year of our Lord one thousand seven hundred and Eighty seven and of the Independence of the United States of America the Twelfth. IN WITNESS whereof We have hereunto subscribed our Names.

Gº WASHINGTON
Presid^t and deputy from Virginia

THE SIGNERS OF THE CONSTITUTION

New Hampshire
John Langdon
Nicholas Gilman

Massachusetts
Nathaniel Gorham
Rufus King

Connecticut
William Samuel Johnson
Roger Sherman

New York
Alexander Hamilton

New Jersey
William Livingston
David Brearley
William Paterson
Jonathan Dayton

Pennsylvania
Benjamin Franklin
Thomas Mifflin
Robert Morris
George Clymer
Thomas Fitzsimmons
Jared Ingersoll
James Wilson
Gouverneur Morris

Delaware
George Read
Gunning Bedford, Jr.
John Dickinson
Richard Bassett
Jacob Broom

Maryland
James McHenry
Daniel of St. Thomas
    Jenifer
Daniel Carroll

Virginia
John Blair
James Madison, Jr.

North Carolina
William Blount
Richard Dobbs Spraight
Hugh Williamson

South Carolina
John Rutledge
Charles Pinckney
Charles Cotesworth
    Pinckney
Pierce Butler

Georgia
William Few
Abraham Baldwin

— Reading No. 5 —

THE VIRGINIA AMENDMENTS, JUNE 27, 1788 *

The bill of rights and limiting amendments adopted by the Virginia convention included most of the amendments proposed in the state conventions which had met previously. The Virginia amendments therefore represent a good summary of the many objections raised to the Constitution throughout the United States.

✓   ✓   ✓

[BILL OF RIGHTS]

That there be a declaration or bill of rights asserting, and securing from encroachment, the essential and un-alienable rights of the people, in some such manner as the following:

1st. That there are certain natural rights, of which men, when they form a social compact, cannot deprive or divest their posterity; among which are the enjoyment of life and liberty, with the means of acquiring, possessing, and protecting property, and pursuing and obtaining happiness and safety.

2d. That all power is naturally invested in, and consequently derived from, the people; that magistrates therefore are their trustees and agents, at all times amenable to them.

3d. That government ought to be instituted for the common benefit, protection, and security of the people; and that the doctrine of non-resistance against arbitrary

---

* Jonathan Elliot, *The Debates in the Several State Conventions.* . . . (5 vols., Washington, 1836-1859), Vol. III, pp. 657-661.

power and oppression is absurd, slavish, and destructive to the good and happiness of mankind.

4th. That no man or set of men are entitled to separate or exclusive public emoluments or privileges from the community, but in consideration of public services, which not being descendible, neither ought the offices of magistrate, legislator, or judge, or any other public office, to be hereditary.

5th. That the legislative, executive, and judicial powers of government should be separate and distinct; and that the members of the two first may be restrained from oppression by feeling and participating in the public burdens, they should, at fixed periods, be reduced to a private station, return into the mass of the people, and the vacancies be supplied by certain and regular elections, in which all or any part of the former members to be eligible or ineligible, as the rules of the Constitution of government and the laws shall direct.

6th. That the elections of representatives in the legislature ought to be free and frequent, and all men having sufficient evidence of permanent common interest with, and attachment to, the community ought to have the right of suffrage; and no aid, charge, tax, or fee can be set, rated, or levied upon the people without their own consent, or that of their representatives, so elected; nor can they be bound by any law to which they have not, in like manner, assented for the public good.

7th. That all power of suspending laws, or the execution of laws, by any authority, without the consent of the representatives of the people in the legislature, is injurious to their rights, and ought not to be exercised.

8th. That in all criminal and capital prosecutions, a man hath a right to demand the cause and nature of his accusation, to be confronted with the accusers and witnesses, to call for evidence, and be allowed counsel in his favor, and to a fair and speedy trial by an impartial jury of his vicinage, without whose unanimous consent he cannot be found guilty, (except in the government of the land and naval forces); nor can he be compelled to give evidence against himself.

9th. That no freeman ought to be taken, imprisoned, or dis-seized of his freehold, liberties, privileges, or franchises, or outlawed, or exiled, or in any manner destroyed, or deprived of his life, liberty, or property, but by the law of the land.

10th. That every freeman restrained of his liberty is entitled to a remedy, to inquire into the lawfulness thereof, and to remove the same, if unlawful, and that such remedy ought not to be denied nor delayed.

11th. That, in controversies respecting property and in suits between man and man, the ancient trial by jury is one of the greatest securities to the rights of the people, and to remain sacred and inviolable.

12th. That every freeman ought to find a certain remedy by recourse to the laws, for all injuries and wrongs he may receive in his person, property, or character. He ought to obtain right and justice freely, without sale, completely and without denial, promptly and without delay; and that all establishments or regulations contravening these rights are oppressive and unjust.

13th. That excessive bail ought not to be required, nor excessive fines imposed, nor cruel and unusual punishments inflicted.

14th. That every freeman has a right to be secure from all unreasonable searches and seizures of his person, his papers, and property; all warrants, therefore, to search suspected places, or seize any freeman, his papers, or property, without information on oath (or affirmation of a person religiously scrupulous of taking an oath) of legal and sufficient cause, are grievous and oppressive; and all general warrants to search suspected places, or to apprehend any suspected person, without specially naming or describing the place or person, are dangerous, and ought not to be granted.

15th. That the people have a right peaceably to assemble together to consult for the common good, or to instruct their representatives; and that every freeman has a right to petition or apply to the legislature for redress of grievances.

16th. That the people have a right to freedom of speech and of writing and publishing their sentiments; that the freedom of the press is one of the greatest bulwarks of liberty and ought not to be violated.

17th. That the people have a right to keep and bear arms; that a well-regulated militia, composed of the body of the people trained to arms, is the proper, natural, and safe defense of a free state; that standing armies, in time of peace, are dangerous to liberty, and therefore ought to be avoided, as far as the circumstances and protection of the community will admit; and that, in all cases, the military should be under strict subordination to, and governed by, the civil authority.

18th. That no soldier in time of peace ought to be quartered in any house without the consent of the owner, and in time of war in such manner only as the law directs.

19th. That any person religiously scrupulous of bearing arms ought to be exempted, upon payment of an equivalent to employ another to bear arms in his stead.

20th. That religion, or the duty which we owe to our Creator, and the manner of discharging it can be directed only by reason and conviction, not by force or violence; and therefore all men have an equal, natural, and unalienable right to the free exercise of religion, according to the dictates of conscience, and that no particular religious sect or society ought to be favored or established, by law, in preference to others.

AMENDMENTS TO THE CONSTITUTION

1st. That each state in the union shall respectively retain every power, jurisdiction, and right which is not by this Constitution delegated to the Congress of the United States, or to the departments of the federal government.

2d. That there shall be one representative for every thirty thousand, according to the enumeration or census mentioned in the Constitution, until the whole number of representatives amounts to two hundred; after which that number shall be continued or increased, as Congress shall direct, upon the principles fixed in the Constitution, by apportioning the representatives of each state to some greater number of people, from time to time, as population increases.

3d. When the Congress shall lay direct taxes or excises, they shall immediately inform the executive power of each state of the quota of such state, according to the census herein directed, which is proposed to be thereby raised; and if the legislature of any state shall pass a law which shall be effectual for raising such quota at the time required by Congress, the taxes and excises laid by Congress shall not be collected in such state.

4th. That the members of the senate and house of representatives shall be ineligible to, and incapable of holding any civil office under the authority of the United States, during the time for which they shall respectively be elected.

5th. That the journals of the proceedings of the senate and house of representatives shall be published at least once in every year, except such parts thereof relating to treaties, alliances, or military operations, as in their judgment, require secrecy.

6th. That a regular statement and account of the receipts and expenditures of public money shall be published at least once a year.

7th. That no commercial treaty shall be ratified without the concurrence of two-thirds of the whole number of the members of the senate; and no treaty ceding, contracting, restraining, or suspending the territorial rights or claims of the United States, or any of them, or their, or any of their rights or claims to fishing in the American seas, or navigating the American rivers, shall be made, but in cases of the most urgent and extreme necessity; nor shall any such treaty be ratified without the concurrence of three-fourths of the whole number of the members of both houses respectively.

8th. That no navigation law, or law regulating commerce, shall be passed without the consent of two-thirds of the members present, in both houses.

9th. That no standing army, or regular troops, shall be raised, or kept up, in time of peace, without the consent of two-thirds of the members present, in both houses.

10th. That no soldier shall be enlisted for any longer term than four years, except in time of war, and then for no longer term than the continuance of the war.

11th. That each state respectively shall have the power to provide for organizing, arming, and disciplining its own militia, whensoever Congress shall omit or neglect to provide for the same. That the militia shall not be subject to martial law, except when in actual service, in time of war, invasion, or rebellion; and, when not in the actual service of the United States, shall be subject only to such fines, penalties, and punishments as shall be directed or inflicted by the laws of its own state.

12th. That the exclusive power of legislation given to Congress over the federal town and its adjacent district, and other places, purchased or to be purchased by Congress of any of the states, shall extend only to such regulations as respect the police and good government thereof.

13th. That no person shall be capable of being president of the United States for more than eight years in any term of sixteen years.

14th. That the judicial power of the United States shall be vested in one supreme court, and in such courts of admiralty as Congress may from time to time ordain and establish in any of the different states. The judicial power shall extend to all cases in law and equity arising under treaties made, or which shall be made, under the authority of the United States; to all cases affecting ambassadors, other foreign ministers, and consuls; to all cases of admiralty and maritime jurisdiction; to controversies to which the United States shall be a party; to controversies between two or more states, and between parties claiming lands under the grants of different states. In all cases affecting ambassadors, other foreign ministers, and consuls, and those in which a state shall be a party, the supreme court shall have original jurisdiction; in all other cases before mentioned, the supreme court shall have appellate jurisdiction, as to matters of law only, except in cases of equity, and of admiralty, and maritime jurisdiction, in which the supreme court shall have appellate jurisdiction both as to law and fact, with such exceptions and under such regulations as the Congress shall make; but the judicial power of the United States shall extend to no case where the cause of action shall have originated before the ratification of the Constitution, except in disputes between states about their territory, disputes between persons claiming lands under the grants of different states, and suits for debts due to the United States.

15th. That, in criminal prosecutions, no man shall be restrained in the exercise of the usual and accustomed right of challenging or excepting to the jury.

16th. That Congress shall not alter, modify, or interfere in the times, places, or manner of holding elections for senators and representatives, or either of them, except when the legislature of any state shall neglect, refuse, or be disabled, by invasion or rebellion, to prescribe the same.

17th. That those clauses which declare that Congress shall not exercise certain powers be not interpreted, in any manner whatsoever, to extend the powers of Congress; but that they be construed either as making exceptions to the specified powers where this shall be the case, or otherwise as inserted merely for greater caution.

18th. That the laws ascertaining the compensation of senators and representatives for their services be postponed in their operation until after the election of representatives immediately succeeding the passing thereof; that excepted which shall first be passed on the subject.

19th. That some tribunal other than the senate be provided for trying impeachments of senators.

20th. That the salary of a judge shall not be increased or diminished during his continuance in office, otherwise than by general regulations of salary, which may take place on a revision of the subject at stated periods of not less than seven years, to commence from the time such salaries shall be first ascertained by Congress.

— Reading No. 6 —

THE BILL OF RIGHTS, 1791

James Madison offered the first version of the Bill of Rights in the house of representatives on June 8, 1789. There was considerable delay and objection, and it was not until September 25 that Congress sent 12 amendments to the president for submission to the state legislatures. The states rejected an amendment dealing with apportionment in the house of representatives and another forbidding senators and representatives to change their salaries until an election had intervened. The 10 amendments composing the Bill of Rights were ratified by the necessary eleventh state, Virginia, on December 15, 1791.

ARTICLE I

Congress shall make no law respecting an establishment of religion, or prohibiting the free exercise thereof; or abridging the freedom of speech, or of the press; or the right of the people peaceably to assemble, and to petition the Government for a redress of grievances.

ARTICLE II

A well regulated Militia, being necessary to the security of a free State, the right of the people to keep and bear Arms, shall not be infringed.

ARTICLE III

No Soldier shall, in time of peace, be quartered in any house, without the consent of the Owner, nor in time of war, but in a manner to be prescribed by law.

ARTICLE IV

The right of the people to be secure in their persons, houses, papers, and effects, against unreasonable searches and seizures, shall not be violated, and no Warrants shall issue, but upon probable cause, supported by Oath or affirmation, and particularly describing the place to be searched, and the persons or things to be seized.

ARTICLE V

No person shall be held to answer for a capital, or otherwise infamous crime, unless on a presentment or indictment of a Grand Jury, except in cases arising in the land or naval forces, or in the Militia, when in actual service in time of War or public danger; nor shall any person be subject for the same offence to be twice put in jeopardy of life or limb; nor shall be compelled in any Criminal Case to be a witness against himself, nor be deprived of life, liberty, or property, without due process of law; nor shall private property be taken for public use, without just compensation.

ARTICLE VI

In all criminal prosecutions, the accused shall enjoy the right to a speedy and public trial, by an impartial jury of the State and district wherein the crime shall have been committed, which district shall have been previously ascertained by law, and to be informed of the nature and cause of the accusation; to be confronted with the witnesses against him; to have compulsory process for obtaining Witnesses in his favor, and to have the Assistance of Counsel for his defence.

ARTICLE VII

In suits at common law, where the value in controversy shall exceed twenty dollars, the right of trial by jury shall be preserved, and no fact tried by a jury shall be otherwise re-examined in any Court of the United States, than according to the rules of the common law.

ARTICLE VIII

Excessive bail shall not be required, nor excessive fines imposed, nor cruel and unusual punishments inflicted.

ARTICLE IX

The enumeration in the Constitution, of certain rights, shall not be construed to deny or disparage others retained by the people.

ARTICLE X

The powers not delegated to the United States by the Constitution, nor prohibited by it to the States, are reserved to the States respectively, or to the people.

BIBLIOGRAPHICAL ESSAY

The basic sources for the making of the Constitution are the debates in the Constitutional Convention and in the state ratifying conventions. The journal, debates, and other materials for the Convention have been edited by Max Farrand, *The Records of the Federal Convention of 1787* (rev. ed., 4 vols., New Haven, 1937). Many documents and most of the debates were published in Charles C. Tansill, ed., *Documents Illustrative of the Formation of the Union of the American States* (Washington, 1927).

The debates in the state ratifying conventions were first printed by Jonathan Elliot in *The Debates in the Several State Conventions* . . . (5 vols., Washington, 1836-1845). The volumes are useful but inadequate. John B. McMaster and Frederick Stone, *Pennsylvania and the Federal Constitution, 1787-1788* (Lancaster, 1888) give a far fuller account of the Pennsylvania debates, and in addition, newspaper and pamphlet material. In 1856, Massachusetts published the journal and a new edition of the debates in the Massachusetts convention. Fortunately, a complete edition of all the material relating to ratification is now under way.

The ratification controversy produced a host of pamphlets, tracts, essays, and newspaper writing ranging all the way from squibs and "recipes" to poetry. The most famous essays are, of course, *The Federalist* papers by Hamilton, Madison, and Jay. There are many editions, but the most scholarly—one reprinted from the contemporary newspapers—is by Jacob E. Cooke (Middletown, Conn., 1961). P. L. Ford published two useful collections: *Pamphlets on the Constitution* (Brooklyn, 1888) and *Essays on the Constitution* (Brooklyn, 1892). Much of the material from these volumes was reprinted by E. H. Scott in *The Federalist and Other Constitutional Papers* (Chicago, 1894). Samuel Bryan's 24 "Essays of Centinel," the most detailed writing by an opponent of ratification, are republished in McMaster and Stone.

Virtually untouched and unread is the mass of material in the newspapers of the time. In the newspapers rather than in the more weighty pamphlets one finds some of the most colorful, vigorous, and significant material for the history of ratification.

By all odds the best detailed study of the writing of the Constitution is Charles Warren's *The Making of the Constitution* (Boston, 1928). Warren goes through the Convention day by day and with great learning discusses the issues involved and, in addition, outlines the development of the Constitution after 1789. The most controversial book ever written about the Constitution is Charles A. Beard's *An Economic Interpretation of the Constitution* (New York, 1913). For a half century it has generated more heat than light and has turned all too few scholars to the detailed study of the period that Beard said was necessary and which he hoped to inspire. A recent example of the book's enduring role as a generator of heat is Robert E. Brown's *Charles Beard and the Constitution: A Critical Analysis of "An Economic Interpretation of the Constitution"* (Princeton, 1956). In his effort to exorcise the Beardian ghost, Brown has often overstated his case. Forrest McDonald's *We the People: The Economic Origins of the Constitution* (Chicago, 1958) has also attacked Beard by offering a differing and far more complex economic interpretation. Lee Benson's *Turner and Beard: American Historical Writing Reconsidered* (Glencoe, Ill., 1960) alleges that Beard confused "economic determinism" with "economic interpretation." At the same time Benson subjects Brown and McDonald's criticisms of Beard to a critical analysis and raises serious questions about their validity.

During the past few years, several people have published articles offering interpretations of the writing of the Constitution, the motives of the Founding Fathers, and the like. With a few exceptions, such articles are based on the "critical" evaluation of monographs. Most of the authors of such articles have two things in common: (1) they make too many careless generalizations; (2) they show little evidence of having read sources such as the debates in the conventions, the newspapers, and collections of letters. For these reasons such articles are of little value in understanding the making of the Constitution. The most recent example is Stanley Elkins and Eric McKitrick, *The Founding Fathers: Young Men of the Revolution* (Service Center for Teachers of History, Publication No. 44, Washington, 1962).

Aside from McMaster and Stone, there are only a few book-length studies of ratification by the states. The two best are Samuel B. Harding, *The Contest Over the Ratification of the Federal Constitution in the State of Massachusetts* (New York, 1896) and Louise Trenholme, *The Ratification of the Federal Constitution in North Carolina* (New York, 1932). Charles E. Miner's *The Ratification of the Federal Constitution by the State of New York* (New York, 1921) is useful, but it is little more than an outline. Hugh Blair Grigsby, *The History of the Virginia Federal Convention of 1788*. . . . (2 vols., Richmond, 1890-1891) has valuable material, but is by no means adequate. Richard P. McCormick's account of ratification in New Jersey in *Experiment in Independence: New Jersey in the Critical Period, 1781-1789* (New Brunswick, 1950) is a model short essay. The most recent study is Jackson Turner Main's *The Antifederalists: Critics of the Constitution, 1781-1788* (Chapel Hill, 1961). Although Main concentrates on the opponents of the Constitution, his book presents the best brief account of the issues involved in each state, and his bibliographical essay is a valuable survey of the secondary and source materials. E. James Ferguson, *The Power of the Purse: A History of American Public Finance, 1776-1790* (Chapel Hill, 1961) is a detailed account of the relationship of economic forces to the political and constitutional history of the period. Merrill Jensen, *The Articles of Confederation* (3rd printing, Madison, 1959) and *The New Nation: A History of the United States During the Confederation, 1781-1789* (New York, 1950) provide a political and constitutional background for the work of the Convention of 1787.

INDEX

VAN NOSTRAND ANVIL BOOKS already published

1 *MAKING OF MODERN FRENCH MIND*—Kohn
2 *THE AMERICAN REVOLUTION*—Morris
3 *THE LATE VICTORIANS*—Ausubel
4 *WORLD IN THE 20th CENTURY*—Rev. Ed. Snyder
5 *50 DOCUMENTS OF THE 20th CENTURY*—Snyder
6 *THE AGE OF REASON*—Snyder
7 *MARX AND THE MARXISTS*—Hook
8 *NATIONALISM*—Kohn
9 *MODERN JAPAN*—Rev. Ed. Tiedemann
10 *50 DOCUMENTS OF THE 19th CENTURY*—Snyder
11 *CONSERVATISM*—Viereck
12 *THE PAPACY*—Corbett
13 *AGE OF THE REFORMATION*—Bainton
14 *DOCUMENTS IN AMERICAN HISTORY*—Morris
15 *CONTEMPORARY AFRICA*—Rev. Ed. Wallbank
16 *THE RUSSIAN REVOLUTIONS OF 1917*—Curtiss
17 *THE GREEK MIND*—Agard
18 *BRITISH CONSTITUTIONAL HISTORY SINCE 1832*—Schuyler
   and Weston
19 *THE NEGRO IN THE U.S.*—Logan
20 *AMERICAN CAPITALISM*—Hacker
21 *LIBERALISM*—Schapiro
22 *THE FRENCH REVOLUTION, 1789-1799*—Gershoy
23 *HISTORY OF MODERN GERMANY*—Snyder
24 *HISTORY OF MODERN RUSSIA*—Kohn
25 *NORTH ATLANTIC CIVILIZATION*—Kraus
26 *NATO*—Salvadori
27 *DOCUMENTS IN U.S. FOREIGN POLICY*—Brockway
28 *AMERICAN FARMERS' MOVEMENTS*—Shannon
29 *HISTORIC DECISIONS OF SUPREME COURT*—Swisher
30 *MEDIEVAL TOWN*—Mundy and Riesenberg
31 *REVOLUTION AND REACTION 1848-1852*—Bruun
32 *SOUTHEAST ASIA AND WORLD TODAY*—Buss
33 *HISTORIC DOCUMENTS OF W. W. I*—Snyder
34 *HISTORIC DOCUMENTS OF W. W. II*—Langsam
35 *ROMAN MIND AT WORK*—MacKendrick
36 *SHORT HISTORY OF CANADA*—Masters
37 *WESTWARD MOVEMENT IN U.S.*—Billington
38 *DOCUMENTS IN MEDIEVAL HISTORY*—Downs
39 *HISTORY OF AMERICAN BUSINESS*—Cochran
40 *DOCUMENTS IN CANADIAN HISTORY*—Talman
41 *FOUNDATIONS OF ISRAEL*—Janowsky
42 *MODERN CHINA*—Rowe
43 *BASIC HISTORY OF OLD SOUTH*—Stephenson
44 *THE BENELUX COUNTRIES*—Eyck
45 *MEXICO AND THE CARIBBEAN*—Hanke
46 *SOUTH AMERICA*—Hanke
47 *SOVIET FOREIGN POLICY, 1917-1941*—Kennan
48 *THE ERA OF REFORM, 1830-1860*—Commager
49 *EARLY CHRISTIANITY*—Bainton
50 *RISE AND FALL OF THE ROMANOVS*—Mazour
51 *CARDINAL DOCUMENTS IN BRITISH HISTORY*—Schuyler and
   Weston
52 *HABSBURG EMPIRE 1804-1918*—Kohn
53 *CAVOUR AND UNIFICATION OF ITALY*—Salvadori
54 *ERA OF CHARLEMAGNE*—Easton and Wieruszowski
55 *MAJOR DOCUMENTS IN AMERICAN ECONOMIC HISTORY,
   Vol. I*—Hacker
56 *MAJOR DOCUMENTS IN AMERICAN ECONOMIC HISTORY,
   Vol. II*—Hacker
57 *HISTORY OF THE CONFEDERACY*—Vandiver
58 *COLD WAR DIPLOMACY*—Graebner
59 *MOVEMENTS OF SOCIAL DISSENT IN MODERN EUROPE*—
   Schapiro
60 *MEDIEVAL COMMERCE*—Adelson
61 *THE PEOPLE'S REPUBLIC OF CHINA*—Buss
62 *WORLD COMMUNISM*—Hook
63 *ISLAM AND THE WEST*—Hitti